A Rookie's Guide To Pool Table Maintenance And Repair is the only book available that completely explains all billiard table maintenance, including slate installation, and game accessories. The book is very good and needed by the industry.

     -Steve Lunsford, Steve Lunsford Corporation, Billiard Slates.

A Rookie's Guide To Pool Table Maintenance And Repair is the most comprehensive source of information concerning billiard table maintenance, cloth, cushion, and slate replacement.

     -Craig Connelly, Connelly Billiard Manufacturing, Inc.

A Rookie's Guide To Pool Table Maintenance And Repair should be required reading for anyone in the business, or anyone wanting to learn anything about pool tables.

A Rookie's Guide To Pool Table Maintenance And Repair is organized in sections. Each is a logical division intended to help readers quickly find their area of interest from dismantling and moving to re-covering a pool table.

A Rookie's Guide To Pool Table Maintenance And Repair expertly explains all aspects of pool table maintenance, accessory maintenance, cloth and cushion replacement, leveling, etc.

A Rookie's Guide To Pool Table Maintenance And Repair, finally, an all-encompassing book for anyone wanting to learn about pool tables.

D1591863

A Rookie's Guide To Pool Table Maintenance And Repair is an accumulation of twenty-five years of empirical and "accepted" knowledge and experience. It is a comprehensive book on the structure of billiard tables, equipment, maintenance, and specifications, which makes it a complete, one-source maintenance book.

A Rookie's Guide To Pool Table Maintenance And Repair is well illustrated with clear figures, and seeded with reference tables and sidebar "WORDS OF EXPERIENCE," "TRICK OF THE TRADE," "CAUTION," and "ON THE LEVEL," tips on making some maintenance procedures easier and safer.

A Rookie's Guide To Pool Table Maintenance And Repair details all aspects of pool table care from simple maintenance to replacing the cloth, and everything in between.

A Rookie's Guide To Pool Table Maintenance And Repair is a handy, concise, and informative pool and billiard guidebook. It is expertly organized and chocked full of maintenance procedures, helpful hints, and pertinent illustrations.

A Rookie's Guide To Pool Table Maintenance And Repair thoroughly covers the structure of pool tables and equipment, as well as their maintenance and specifications.

A Complete Guide to Pool Table Maintenance & Repair was written in an easy to read, straightforward language.

A Complete Guide to Pool Table Maintenance & Repair, one word: Excellent!

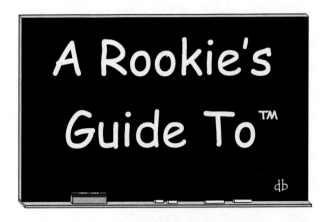

POOL TABLE
MAINTENANCE & REPAIR

A MANUAL TO ASSEMBLE, RE-COVER, RE-CUSHION, LEVEL, AND REPAIR ANY POOL TABLE

Mose Duane

Phoenix Billiards

6133 W. Port-au-Prince Lane
Glendale, AZ 85306
(rookies-guide.com)

The purpose of this manual is to educate and entertain. It is designed to provide information in regard to the subject matter covered. It is sold with the understanding that the publisher and author are not engaged in rendering legal or professional services. If legal or other expert assistance is required, the services of a competent professional should be sought. Although the author and publisher have used care and diligence in the preparation, and made every effort to ensure the accuracy and completeness of information contained in this manual, we assume no responsibility for errors, inaccuracies, omissions, or any inconsistency herein. Any slights to people, places, or organizations are unintentional. The author and publisher shall have neither liability nor responsibility to any person or entity with respect to any loss or damage caused, or alleged to be caused, directly or indirectly by the information contained in this manual. This manual is sold as a revised version of an earlier book titled "The Billiard Guidebook." If you do not agree with the terms in this paragraph, please return this manual, with proof of purchase, within thirty days of its purchase for a full refund of the price of the book.

Illustrated by the author
Cover by Erika A. Diehl, www.porchpuppyonline.com
Printed by Print Partner, Tempe, Arizona, United States of America

Publisher's Cataloging-in-Publication
(Provided by Quality Books, Inc.)

Duane, Mose.
   A rookie's guide to pool table maintenance & repair :
a manual to assemble, re-cover, re-cushion, level, and
repair any pool table / Mose Duane.
   p. cm.
   Includes index.
   LCCN 2004098287
   ISBN 0-9678089-8-7

   1. Billiards--Equipment and supplies--Maintenance and
repair.   I. Title. II. Title: Pool table maintenance
& repair. III. Title: Pool table maintenance and repair.

GV899.D83 2005   794.72'028'4
                           QBI04-200521

Contents

CONTENTS iii

CONTENTS

Words of Experience

Early one fall morning, in Columbus, Indiana, I got a phone call from a guy named John who lived in Bloomington, Indiana.

"I was given a pool table," he said. "What's the best way to get it upstairs?"

"Hire me," I answered.

He laughed then told me to have at it.

The next day my helper, Wiley Turner, and I drove to Bloomington. John's house was a nice, new but rustic, three-story home tucked among the golden autumn trees of southern Indiana's famous university town. Snow covered the rolling ground in patches, making the house look even quainter.

John was young, between twenty and twenty-five, had shoulder length hair and a stubble of beard. He wore a T-shirt and new blue jeans with holes in the knees.

The table was an old coin-op with a unicabinet and one-piece slate. It sit on its side at the bottom of an impossible looking, twisting staircase.

I looked at the stairs, the table, and then at John.

"I have help," he said.

Upstairs four or five guys were setting up various musical instruments.

"You guys play in a band?" I asked.

"We try," John answered.

Wiley and I dismantled the table, and with the help of the crew from upstairs, we carried it outside and down the icy, sloping yard to the back of the house. From there, we passed it, piece by piece, straight up to the second floor balcony. We then passed it, again straight up, from the second floor balcony to the third floor balcony and through the sliding glass doors into a spacious room that overlooked the deep, tree-filled gorge behind the house.

After Wiley and I assembled and leveled the table, I handed John the bill.

"Whoa," he said. "It seems like my guys and I did most of the carrying."

"You're paying for what we know, not what we did," I answered. "After all you guys were stuck at the bottom of the stairs."

"Fair enough," he laughed. He then signed the check, John Melloncamp.

Later, I asked my daughter if she had ever heard of him.

"He's a local singer," she said. "But not very well-known."

You never know who's going to become famous.

Introduction

This book is a shortened, slightly revised, and greatly reformatted version of *The Billiard Guidebook*, my original manual on pool table maintenance. In this version, I have removed all references to playing the game and buying or selling a pool table, concentrating entirely on maintenance and repair of tables and some accessories. I have covered playing and buying or selling in greater detail in their own books, *A Rookie's Guide to Playing Winning Pool,* and *A Rookie's Guide to Buying and Selling a Pool Table*.

As stated in *The Billiard Guidebook*, the game of pool must be one of man's most brilliantly devised sports. It is a sport that can be cherished socially or privately, by one or several, in public or in the seclusion of one's home. The game is so simple that a novice can play and thoroughly enjoy it. Yet, it is so complicated–a half sphere imparting motion upon a sphere, which in turn must travel a perfectly flat surface, strike another sphere and send it in a precise predetermined direction, often rebounding from a rubber cushion before it reaches its destination–that a novice can't fully appreciate and the most talented masters frequently make miscalculations and mistakes, and the enormous disparity between the novice and master is incalculable. It is somewhere in that vastness of ability that most players reside, it is that disparity that makes the game so fascinating, and it is no doubt a major reason for the game's current popularity. Pool tables have been around for hundreds of years, but never were they embraced into our homes as exuberantly as they are today. They are displacing formal dining and living rooms, and enhancing dens, bedrooms, basements, lofts, patios, and garages. This explosive popularity of pool tables has made them a cultural phenomenon that will carry well into the future.

However, a couple significant problems have arisen with this expansive popularity, which need to be addressed. First is the inability of consumers to recognize the difference, except in price, between cheap tables and expensive ones. The average consumer cannot tell if a table is poorly constructed, well constructed, or moderately constructed and priced high. From appearance, it is sometimes difficult to tell if a table has been engineered to last a hundred years or a hundred hours. The second problem is that of maintenance and standards, which are thrown upon the consumer with little or continually changing guidelines, if any at all.

For maintenance, few consumers have the experience or expertise to do any more than brush the bed cloth, and most don't realize there is a right way and wrong way to do even that.

A few specifications are required by regulating bodies like the Billiard Congress of America (BCA) to qualify for tournament play. The rest, however, are do-as-you-may, or are standards that are simply accepted as fact by the industry, or changed to meet their present needs.

Many consumers have little idea what these standards are or how to perform more than basic maintenance. And, except for a reluctant installer or salesperson, the consumer had no place to get the information, until *The Billiard Guidebook*, and now of course, this book.

Further, most consumers believe that anything beyond the general maintenance of the table cloth has to be done by a professional pool table installer. Nothing could be farther from the truth. Anyone having the desire to learn and do more can, and has come to the right source. ***A Rookie's Guide to Pool Table Maintenance and Repair*** is an accumulation of my thirty (plus) years of empirical and "accepted" knowledge and experience. Although straightforward, it is a comprehensive book covering the structure of pool tables, equipment, maintenance, and some specifications. Most other books currently on the market were written by players and involve aspects of playing only, or fundamentals, rules, history, and a limited amount of basic "keep it clean" maintenance. This book's major thrust is detailing all aspects of pool table care, from simple maintenance, to replacing the cloth and cushions, to repairing a cracked slate, including segments on dismantling, moving, assembling, leveling, etc. The book is well illustrated with clear figures, and seeded with reference tables and sidebar "WORDS OF EXPERIENCE," "ON THE LEVEL," "TRICK OF THE TRADE," and "CAUTION" tips on making some maintenance procedures easier, safer, and (hopefully) a little more fun.

For anyone not acquainted with frequently used pool or billiard terms, a short glossary has been placed at the end of the book. Take a few minutes to scan any unfamiliar terms. It will make reading much easier.

Reading this book from front to back is not necessary. Those interested in simply "getting the job done" can take full advantage of the table of contents and read only what is of concern.

For those interested in reading the book from cover to cover, some sentences, paragraphs, or ideas of one chapter may be repeated in another. This is necessary and serves two purposes. One, it reinforces significant information, and two, it insures that everyone reading only the chapter they are interested in will not miss any information that might be vital to them or their endeavors.

Also, I'd like to a word, or so, on the quality of workmanship. I wholeheartedly uphold the adages that anything worth doing is worth doing right, and a person's character can be judged by what he or she does when no one is watching. I am appalled when I am called to repair someone else's sloppy work simply because they didn't want to take the time to do the job right to begin with. On the other hand, I feel a certain amount of pride to be associated with the mechanic, if only by industry, when I come upon a job he or she has done well. So, come on, whether you're doing a job for yourself or for someone else, do your level best. It *will* pay dividends in the long run.

And, finally, if anyone feels anything important has been left out of this book, or was not thoroughly and clearly expounded upon, please feel free to write or e-mail (md@rookies-guide.com). Usable suggestions will be rewarded with a free copy of the next revision.

Enjoy.

Mose Duane

WORDS OF EXPERIENCE

I was introduced to the world of pool at the local Boy's Club in Columbus, Indiana at an impressionable age of ten or so. They had one 9-foot table that was always in desperate need of repairs because no one seemed willing or capable of doing the work. Imagine a ten-year-old even considering the lack of maintenance on anything, let alone a game he was just introduced to. But there I was, learning to play on a table with more ruts and valleys than a golf course. In spite of that, I learned enough about playing during those early years to later hustle the game when I was in the army at Fort Campbell, Kentucky, and then in College at Indiana University. However, as strong as I thought I was at IU, I could never beat the long-armed, long-legged IU basketball star and later Indiana Pacer's 1974-75 season's most valuable player, George McGinnis. Along with his magic touch, there wasn't a shot he couldn't reach.

In 1972, my then partner and lifelong friend "Indy" Turner and I opened a twenty-five-table poolroom we called The Velvet Rail in Columbus, Indiana. With the guidance of old timers like Art Schmidt of A.E. Schmidt Billiards, Paul Huebler of Huebler Cues, Gordon Hart of Viking Cues, BCA hall of fame inductee Minnesota Fats, and a local pool player named Fred Perry, Indy and I were quickly educated on the important phases of the pool industry: playing, table maintenance, self-control of being self-employed, and of course hustling the game. It was a crash course of on-the-job-training.

(continued)

WORDS OF EXPERIENCE (CONTINUED)

Indy has since moved on to the wonderful world of casino management in California.

I stayed with pool, first in Indiana then twenty years in Phoenix. I have made or refurbished hundreds of tables, and have moved, re-covered, re-cushioned, and refinished literally thousands of others in those years. I can look at a table and tell its general history including how many nuts, bolts, and screws it takes to hold it together.

Pool is a game of which I have made a profession. It has been good to me. Now I have twenty-five (plus) years of pool and pool table knowledge, a pocket full of change (a small pocket), and feel obligated to give something back. My contribution then is this book. It can cut, if not hours, days, or months, then certainly years, off the learning curve of anyone inclined to follow its instructions.

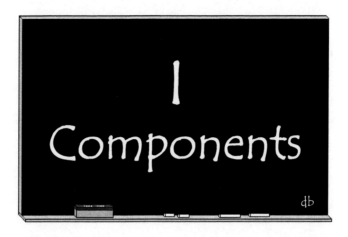

1
Components

Components are all the parts that go together to make a complete pool table. This section describes each component, the materials used in its construction, its function, and if possible its specifications.

Pool table components are constructed from a wide range of materials, including hardwoods, softwoods, plywood, particle board, sheet metal, leather, nuts, bolts, and screws. These materials range from expensive to inexpensive. The advantages of expensive materials are obvious in their appearance, durability, and quality. Their disadvantage is, of course, expense. Tables made of expensive hardware can cost from a few to several thousand dollars, depending on material and the extent of their carvings, inlays, and the craftsmanship that went into the table. Table components constructed from inexpensive materials lack in playability and durability, but have the advantage of bringing new tables into millions of homes that would not otherwise have one, although a used high-quality table may be a better value.

Governing boards like the Billiard Congress of America (BCA) have certain dimensional specifications they require before considering a table to be regulation. Other dimensions are not specified or standardized, they are simply accepted de facto by the industry. I measured hundreds of tables to get the specifications presented in this section. Some dimensions hold true on most tables, others are averages, but all are what I consider to be the best for each particular function.

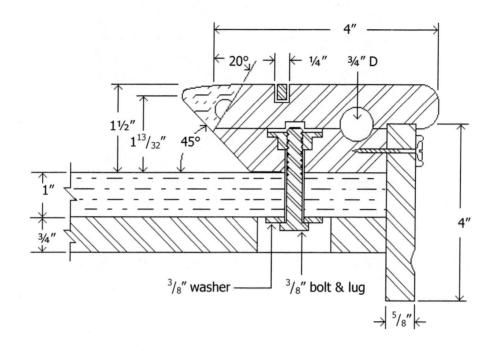

Common flat rail dimensions

IN THIS SECTION

RAILS

There are three kinds of pool table rails commonly used today—T-rails, flat rails, and detachable (coin-operated table) rails (Figure 1-1). One kind is not necessarily better than the others, although detachable rails are generally found on tables in which the rails are not connected to the slate, making them inferior from a playability standpoint, and I like the solid rebound of a good flat rail.

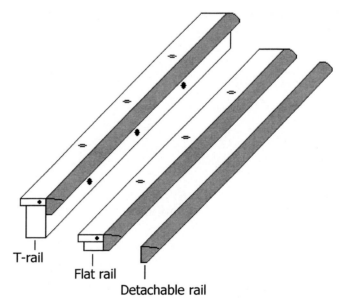

T-rail

Flat rail

Detachable rail

Figure 1-1 *Rails*

Top quality rails are made from select hardwoods that give the table a lively and solid playing characteristic. Some are finished woods, while others are laminated with plastic.

Although some quality rails have durable laminates over hardwoods, which makes a good-looking, functional rail, other lower quality rails are constructed from softwoods and particle boards, and use inexpensive, paper-thin plastics that look good for a while, but are subject to peeling and skinning.

On The Level

A while back, I gave my bill to a doctor, for moving and re-covering his table.

"Jesus," he said, and clearly looked annoyed. "You make more money than I do."

I looked at him and smiled. "What's your point, Doc? I would imagine lots of people make more money than you."

"Yes, but I'm a . . . I mean you're just a . . ." Stumbling for words, he tramped off to get his check book.

You gotta love it!

Three problems develop with the use of softwood and particle board rails. First and foremost is the apparent inability of these materials to hold glue. Laminates and cushions may peel or sag leaving either ugly rails with blisters and bubbles, or cushions that will not rebound properly. Second, these materials are not capable of holding screws or nails over time. Rails become loose, aprons fall off, pockets become detached, and so on. Third, instead of the feather strip (discussed later in this chapter) compressing to hold the cloth the grove opens, allowing the cloth to pull away, often permanently damaging the rail.

T-RAILS

T-rails are most often found on older tables. They are usually constructed by bonding three pieces of hardwood—the top rail, the tacking strip, and the base—together in, more or less, a T shape (Figure 1-2).

The top rail is made from a decorative wood, such as rosewood, ash, oak, mahogany, and so forth. Occasionally the top rail is made of a low-grade softwood or particle board and laminated with a high quality (usually wood grain) plastic, like Formica.

The tacking strip and base are most likely made of poplar. T-rails are attached with bolts from the side, screwing into lugs that have been leaded into the slate. This system of attachment is one of the oldest, but certainly not the easiest, cheapest, or best.

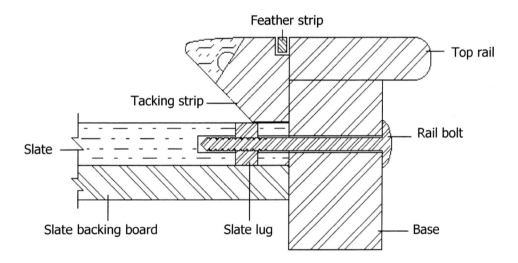

Figure 1-2 *T-rail*

T-rail bolts can be hex-head with standard threads, but most antique tables have a nonstandard, thrust-head bolt with two holes that accepts a fork type tool instead of a standard wrench or socket (Figure 1-3). This tool can be ordered from most pool table supplies stores.

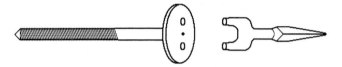

Figure 1-3 *T-rail bolt and tool*

After installation, the bolt heads are hidden with either individual ornamental rosettes or a decorative apron that covers the entire rail base, including the bolts (Figure 1-4).

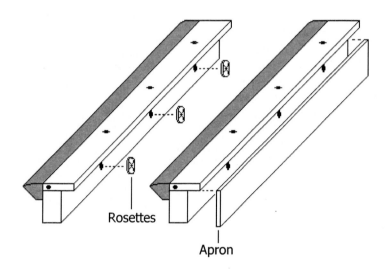

Rosettes

Apron

Figure 1-4 *Apron or rosettes hide the rail bolts*

FLAT RAILS

Flat rails are usually constructed by bonding two pieces of wood together—top rail and base—but can be cut from one block of wood. The top rails of high quality tables are made from an appealing hardwood like rosewood, ash, oak, maple, etc., and the base from an unappealing hardwood such as poplar. Less quality rails could have a top rail laminated with a good quality plastic, but underneath it can be made from almost anything: softwoods, particle board, pressed fiberboard, or some combination, with the base also made from a similar inferior material.

Quality flat rails are attached to the table with rail bolts that penetrate up through the slate and into the rail, which has been equipped with lugs (Figure 1-5), which are imbedded in the rails between the top rail and the base to create a solid attachment.

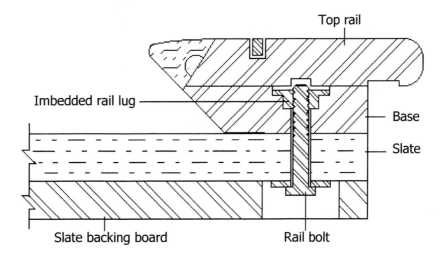

Figure 1-5 *Flat rail*

Generally, flat rails are the better of the three kinds—flat, T, and detachable—because of the positive bottom attachment to the slate. However, some manufacturers bypass the use of lugs altogether by using large wood screws or lag screws. In time, these can become loose, causing a weak connection. Other manufacturers use a flat lug that is screwed to the bottom of the rail with small wood screws. The lugs are only as solid as the wood and screws that hold them (Figure 1-6).

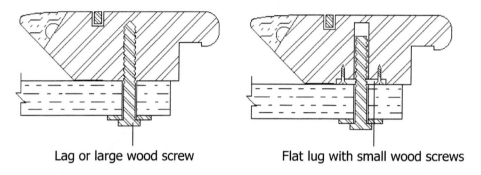

Lag or large wood screw   Flat lug with small wood screws

Figure 1-6 Wood screw attachments

The ends of some flat rails are cut square to accept leather pockets or rail castings (rail 1 in Figure 1-7), while others are mitered to fit together much like a picture frame (rail 2 in Figure 1-7). Squared rail ends allow exposed leather pockets and mitered ends (and rail castings) allow pockets or pocket liners to be attached inside the rail assembly. The converging joints of mitered rails are often covered with a plastic or metal trim.

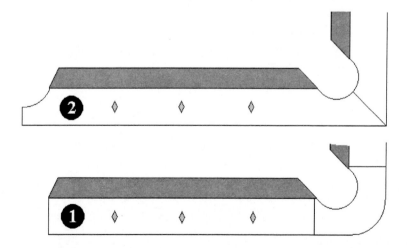

Figure 1-7 *Mitered and squared rails*

Aprons

Some T-rails and all flat rails have an apron to hide the edge of the frame and slate (Figure 1-8). Aprons are either glued permanently to the base, are screwed onto the base or frame, or are attached with metal brackets or wood blocks (see Chapter 8). Except for rails with leather pockets, aprons are joined at the corner with plastic or metal apron corners, and rails are joined with rail caps or castings.

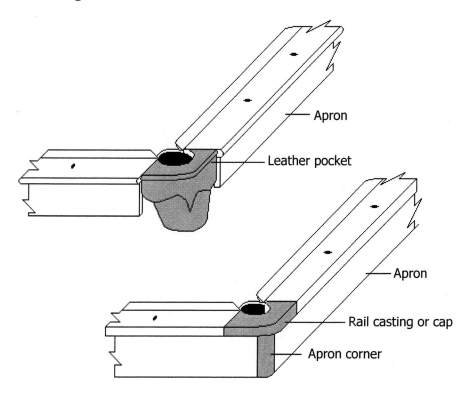

Figure 1-8 *Flat rails with apron*

The length of an apron should be the same as the rail that it is attached to. The apron's width can be anything that adds to the appearance of the pool table but should hide the edge of the slate and frame. Usually, though, narrow aprons are 3 to 4 inches wide, while wide aprons are 6 to 8 inches wide.

The apron's thickness varies from $^1/_4$ to $^3/_4$ inch, and is of no structural significance.

DETACHABLE RAILS

Detachable rails are generally found on coin-operated tables (Figure 1-9), although a few "home-style" tables also have them. A detachable rail is simply a wooden (tacking) strip with cushion rubber and facings glued to it; it is that portion of the assembly covered with billiard cloth. The top rail is permanently (more or less) attached to the frame, thereby becoming part of the cabinet.

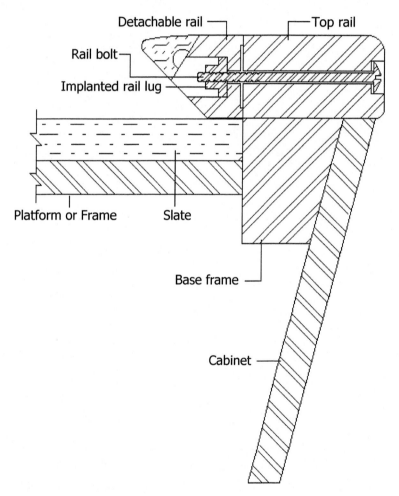

Figure 1-9 *Detachable rail*

Generally, the detachable part of the rail is attached to the top rail in one of three ways: side mount, bottom mount, or metal clip (Figure 1-10).

The most common is the side mount rail that has three or four long bolts (or screws, which are ineffective) that penetrate the width of the top rail and screw into the detachable portion of the rail. The bottom mount rail has an L shaped tacking strip that slides beneath the top rail and is secured from the bottom. The metal clip mount rail has an unusual metal fastener that slides into the middle of the top rail allowing the bottom to hinge beneath the base where it is fastened. The bottom and metal clip mounts are becoming rare but some still exist. They are usually found on home-style tables.

The advantage of the detachable rail method over the T-rail or flat rail is the ease in which an owner can disassemble the table to move or re-cover it. The disadvantage is that detachable rail tables are built with undersize slate that extends only to the edge of the rail; the rail is attached to the frame instead of the slate. The problem with this system is a rail assembly that allows poor ball action.

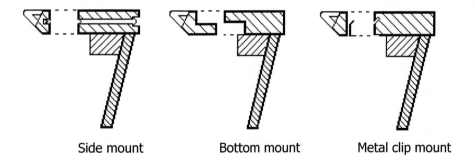

Side mount   Bottom mount   Metal clip mount

Figure 1-10 *Detachable mounts*

RAIL DIMENSIONS

Some rail widths are as narrow as 2 inches while others are as wide as 8, depending on manufacturer and style of the table (Figure 1-11).

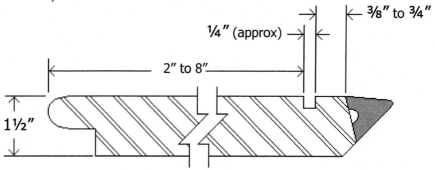

Figure 1-11 *Common rail widths*

Rail lengths (Figure 1-12) vary somewhat from manufacturer to manufacturer, but not by much.

Rails must fit within the constraints of the playing field size, so they must be consistent in their length. However, inconsistencies do occur between tables because no set dimensions for leather pocket setbacks, length of drop pocket castings, or length of miters exist. The further the corner pockets are set away from the table the longer the rails must be—if the setback changes, the rail length must also change, and vice versa (see Chapter 2).

Rail lengths are figured by measuring that part of the rail covered with cloth; that is the measurement that ultimately determines the size of the playing field of the table.

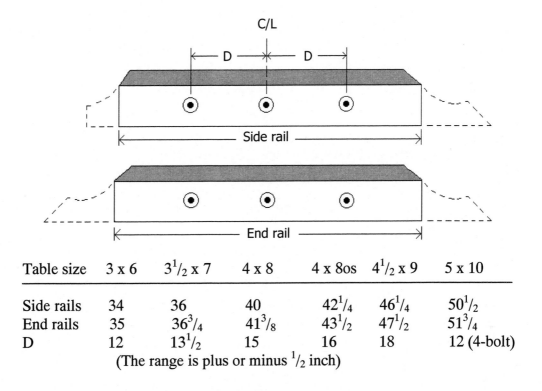

Table size	3 x 6	$3^1/_2$ x 7	4 x 8	4 x 8os	$4^1/_2$ x 9	5 x 10
Side rails	34	36	40	$42^1/_4$	$46^1/_4$	$50^1/_2$
End rails	35	$36^3/_4$	$41^3/_8$	$43^1/_2$	$47^1/_2$	$51^3/_4$
D	12	$13^1/_2$	15	16	18	12 (4-bolt)

(The range is plus or minus $^1/_2$ inch)

Figure 1-12 *Common rail lengths and rail bolt spacing in inches*

RAIL BOLTS

The hardware that holds the rail assembly to the table is the rail bolts or screws (often called hanger bolts). There are three types of rail bolts.

1. T-rail bolts pass through the side of the rail's base and fasten into lugs implanted in the slate (see Figure 1-2).

2. Flat rail bolts go up through the bottom of the table bed (usually penetrating the slate) to fasten into lugs in the rails (see Figure 1-5).

3. Detachable rail bolts pass through the side of the top rail into lugs affixed in the detachable rail (see Figure 1-9).

Lag bolts or wood screws used for rails bolts or lugs simply screw into the bottom of the rail, and most are ineffective.

All rail bolts or screws should be locked with lock washers.

The length of the rail and the number of rail bolts used determines spacing or distance between rail bolts. Typically a three-bolt, 4 x 8 table rail will have rail bolts that are approximately 16 inches on center, with the middle bolt placed in the middle of the rail (Figure 1-12). The pattern for a four-bolt, 4 x 8 table rail will be approximately 12 inches on center, starting 6 inches on both sides of the center of the rail.

CUSHION RUBBER

Quality cushion rubber is molded from 100 percent pure gum rubber. Some cheaper cushions are extruded rubber or synthetics, or molded rubber diluted with fillers.

The two most common cushions are the triangular shaped K-66 and U-23 (Figure 1-13).

K-66 profile is a high-speed cushion used on most commercial and home-style tables. U-23 profile is a medium speed rubber and is used on most coin-operated, and some home-style tables. Although the two cushion types may look the same, they can be distinguished by their size.

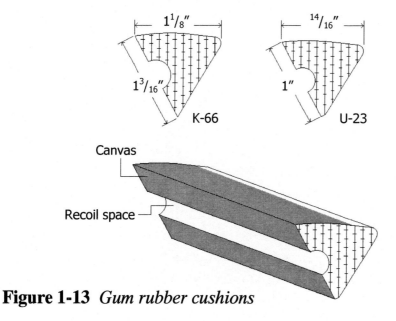

Figure 1-13 *Gum rubber cushions*

K-66 is usually $1^3/_{16}$ inches high by $1^1/_8$ inches wide (back to nose), and U-23 is usually 1 inch high by $^{14}/_{16}$ inches wide. Canvas is molded to the back of most cushion rubber to give it a bonding surface, and to the top to control speed, accuracy, and consistency of ball rebound.

Tables equipped with a non-gum and non-conforming profile rubber should be re-cushioned with their specific rubber. The availability of such rubber depends on the age of the table and the manufacturer. However, it is often possible to re-cut the angle of the rail to accept either U-23 or K-66 profiles (see Chapter 22).

Cushion Height

The critical dimension of a rail is the height of the cushion nose above the playing surface. The cushion nose is that part of the cushion that makes contact with the ball.

When the cushion is at the correct height (rail 1 in Figure 1-14), the nose should be between 61 and 64 percent of the ball height (BCA says $62^1/_2$ percent plus or minus 1 percent).

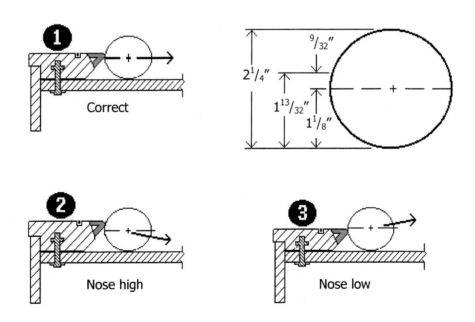

Figure 1-14 *Cushion nose height for 2¼ inch balls*

If the cushion nose is too high, the ball will be forced down onto the slate making the rebound dull and slow (rail 2 in Figure 1-14). If the cushion nose is too low, the ball will be propelled up causing it to hop as it rebounds (rail 3 in Figure 1-14).

Cushion nose height is determined according to the game ball size. The actual rail thickness and cushion attachment angle do not have to be any set dimensions as long as the cushion nose height remains constant. That is, if the thickness of a rail varies then the angle at which the cushion is attached must also vary, and of course, vice versa. However, most rails using full profile (K-66) cushions have dimensions similar to those in Figure 1-15.

	Pool	Snooker 1	Snooker 2	Carom 1	Carom 2
(A)	$1^{1}/_{2}$	$1^{1}/_{2}$	$1^{7}/_{16}$	$1^{1}/_{2}$	$1^{9}/_{16}$
(B)	110°	98°	110°	122°	110°
(C)	$1^{13}/_{32}$	$1^{21}/_{64}$	$1^{21}/_{64}$	$1^{31}/_{64}$	$1^{31}/_{64}$
Ball Size	$2^{1}/_{4}$	$2^{1}/_{8}$	$2^{1}/_{8}$	$2^{3}/_{8}$	$2^{3}/_{8}$

Figure 1-15 *Common rail thickness and cushion heights in inches*

CUSHION FACINGS

Facings are attached to the ends of the cushion and rail to protect them and the rail cloth from excessive wear (Figure 1-16). Facings also deaden the ball's rebound when it is struck, which forces the ball into the pocket. Most facings are laminated rubber and canvas, or cork.

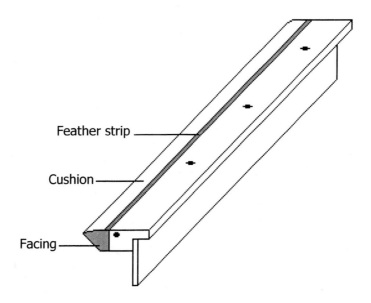

Figure 1-16 *Facing*

FEATHER STRIPS

Feather strips are long thin pieces of wood or plastic used to securely wedge the rail cloth into the top of the rail (Figure 1-17). Feather strips are as long as the rail and fit, along with the rail cloth, into a grove in the top rail.

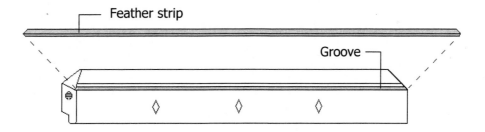

Figure 1-17 *Feather strip*

SIGHTS

Sights (Figure 1-18) can be inlaid into the top rail with a variety of materials. Some older tables have ivory sights, but the most common material is abalone mother-of-pearl, or plastic that resembles mother-of-pearl. Inexpensive tables may have ink-screened sights, or upholsterers' tacks, or cover plates that hide the rail bolts that penetrate the top rail in roughly the sight area. (See Chapter 3, Figure 3-6 for sight spacing.)

Whatever the material, sights were originally strategically located on the rails for aiming purposes. There is a mathematical scheme called *The Diamond System* that can be used to figure angles for bank shots using the sights. The process was originally intended for carom play but works well for any kind of pool table or game. The system employs the application of english and immediate mental calculations during a shot (which is extreme exertion for most of us) and is, therefore, generally ignored. For more information, The Diamond System is explained in several "how to make shots" books and the Billiard Congress of America's (BCA) official rules book. BCA's booklet can be purchased from most pool table supply stores, phoenix**billiards**.com, or directly from: *Billiard Congress of America, 4345 Beverly Street, Colorado Springs, CO 80918*

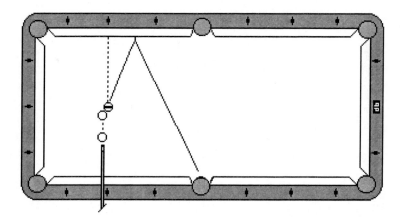

Figure 1-18 *Rail Sights*

POCKETS

Standard pool tables have two kinds of ball retrieval systems. One is a system of six individual pockets that trap the balls in six different locations around the table. The other is a ball return in which the balls are sent to a collection box at the end or side of the table.

Pockets are either exposed leather with leather or knitted webbing, or are molded leather, rubber, or plastic mounted on the interior or the table, behind the aprons. A ball return system consists of pocket liners, gully boots, and gully return tracks.

KNIT POCKETS

Knit pockets are rare, found mostly on antique snooker tables, but they can be on any table and are still available. The only difference between a knitted pocket and a leather pocket is the webbing—one is knitted from a heavy twine and the other is cut from leather.

LEATHER POCKETS

Although some leather pockets are molded to fit inside a boxed rail assembly like rubber or plastic pockets, most are made to hang on the outside of the table (Figure 2-1). They become an aesthetic part of the table, an enhancement of its overall charm or beauty. Attractive hand-tooled leathers, died in various pastel colors with fringe trimmings to match, and inlaid with suede, snake skins, imitation animal skins, and billiard cloth, are designed to coordinate the table with any room decor. Leather pockets are more handsome today then ever.

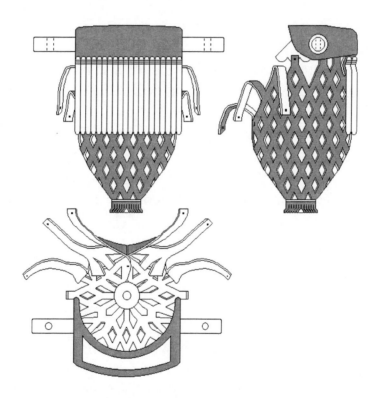

Figure 2-1 *Leather pocket*

Each leather (or knit) pocket consists of five parts: top leather, iron, inside trim, fringe tassel (or leather shield), and webbing (Figure 2-2).

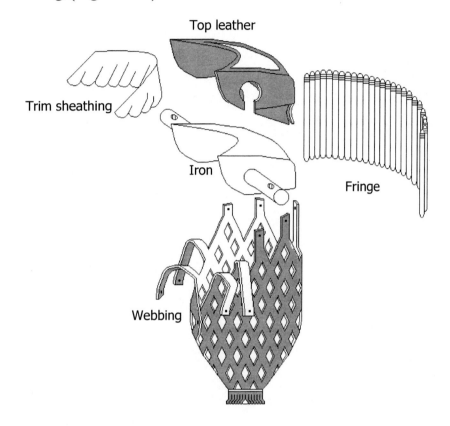

Figure 2-2 *Leather pocket components*

The top leather is formed onto the U shaped irons to make the upper portion of the pocket, and provide a firm means of attachment. The webbing is sewn or riveted onto the top leather beneath the iron. Inside leather trim/sheathing covers the rivets on the inside, and cotton or nylon tassels (or leather shield) do the same for the outside. The webbing connects to the table by tabs that are part of the webbing.

Pocket irons are normally cast from iron or aluminum, but some cheaper versions are now being made of plastic. Lugs that fasten the pocket to the rail are part of the casting. These lugs are drilled and tapped, and are attached to the rail by bolts that penetrate the rail from the bottom. The two most common irons are the #6 and #3

Number 6 Irons

Number 6 leather pocket irons are by far the most commonly used. Number 6 irons have cylindrical lugs that insert into holes in the ends of the rails (Figure 2-3).

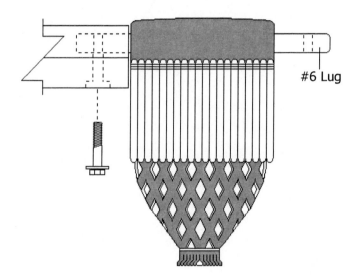

#6 Lug

Figure 2-3 *Number 6 iron lugs*

The #6 iron lugs are bolted into place with either $^5/_{16}$ inch hex-head bolts with flat washers, or $^5/_{16}$ inch countersunk flathead machine screws (approximately $1^1/_2$ inches long for flat rails and 4 inches long for T-rails).

The dimensions for lugs and bolt holes are the same for center pockets and corner pockets (Figure 2-4), and for T-rails and flat rails. The bolt holes and are drilled slightly larger ($^7/_{16}$) than the bolt size to allow easy assembly.

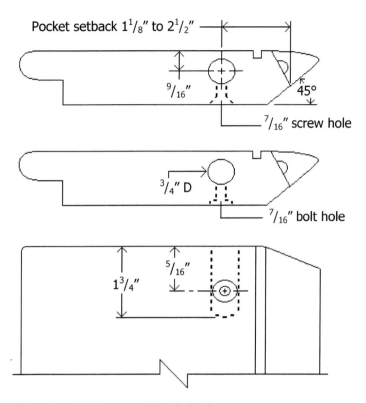

Figure 2-4 *Number 6 iron and bolt holes*

The setback dimension in Figure 2-4 is shown only as a reference. The dimension is ultimately set by the playing field size in relation to the length of the rails for corner pockets, and the size of the pocket cutout in the slate for side pockets (see Figure 2-7).

Number 3 Irons

Number 3 leather pocket irons (Figure 2-5) are commonly found on older T-rail tables, but a few new tables and flat rail tables also have them. The lugs of #3 irons are exposed at the top of the rail and are chromed or brass plated.

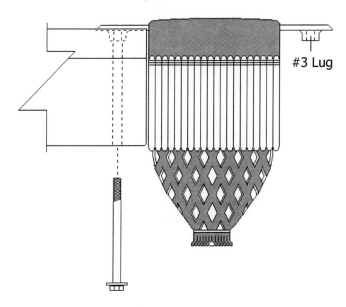

Figure 2-5 *Number 3 iron lugs*

These irons have a stiffening insert below the flat lug to help support it. The top rail must be slotted to receive the insert. The corners of this insert will be square on older #3 irons and rounded on newer ones. With a little modification on the top rail both styles can be interchanged.

A $^5/_{16}$-inch bolt is used to secure the pocket iron, but a $^7/_{16}$-inch hole is drilled through the rail to allow for ease of assembly (pocket bolts are approximately $1^1/_2$ inches long for flat rails, and 4 inches long for T-rails). The dimensions for lugs and bolt holes are the same for center pockets and corner pockets (Figure 2-6), and T-rails and flat rails.

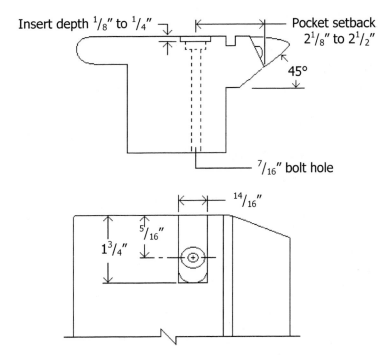

Figure 2-6 *Number 3 iron and bolt holes*

The setback dimension in Figure 2-6 is shown only as a reference. The dimension is ultimately set by the playing field size in relation to the length of the rails for corner pockets, and the size of the pocket cutout in the slate for side pockets (Figure 2-7).

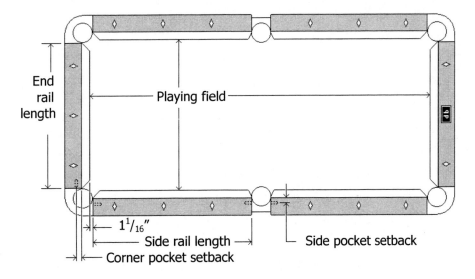

Figure 2-7 *Pocket setbacks*

Over the years an assortment of pocket iron designs have been manufactured, each with its own letter or number designation. Some differ enough in appearance—square lugs, flat backs, etc.—that telling them apart is not difficult. Others, however, look very similar and at first glance appear to be interchangeable but, without some rebuilding of the rails, they are not (Figure 2-8).

Number 6 and #5 irons appear to be the same and are somewhat interchangeable on flat rails that are adjustable, but are generally not interchangeable on T-rails. However, the #5 iron is thinner at the lug, and was made for a very narrow rail. Number 3 and #G irons also appear to be the same. Nevertheless, the #3 has a wider opening, $4^1/_2$ versus $4^1/_8$ inches, and wider lugs, $1^1/_8$ versus 1 inch, and is not interchangeable with the #G. The Hollywood and Wenco (both rare these days) can also be interchanged with a little work, but the appearance of the finished pocket is quiet different: squared back verses rounded, etc.

If possible, it is usually easier, and often cheaper, to simply have old irons re-leathered instead of trying to replace them.

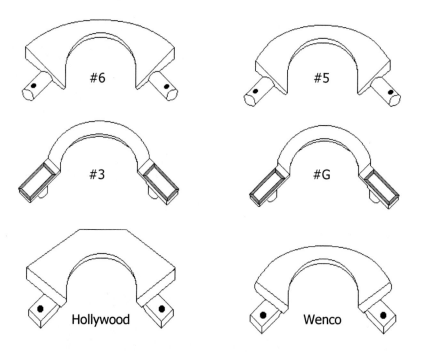

Figure 2-8 *Common pocket irons*

POCKET OPENINGS

Pocket openings refer to the widest distance from cushion to cushion across the entrance to the pocket for pool tables. For snooker tables, it refers to the distance across the opening where the cushions intersect with the slate pocket cutouts (dimension A in Figures 2-9 and 2-10).

Angle B for pool tables (rail 1 in Figure 2-9 and 10) is not a specification but an empirical guideline. It will of course change if dimension A changes, and vice versa.

Radius B for snooker tables (rail 2 in Figure 2-9 and 10) is also an empirical guideline, but does not change even if dimension A changes.

Radius C in Figure 2-9 and 10 is the radius of the pocket and finished pocket cutout, not necessarily the radius of the slate pocket cutout (see Figure 2-11).

Dimension D, however, remains constant and the interior edge of the slate cutout is usually in line with the nose of the cushions.

Center Pocket

Rail 1 of Figure 2-9 represents the side pocket of a pool table, and rail 2, a snooker table.

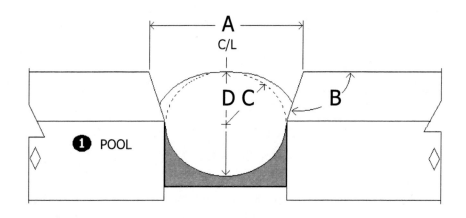

	Pool	Coin-operated	Snooker
(A)	$5^3/_8$" - $5^5/_8$"	5" - $5^1/_2$"	$4^1/_{16}$" - $4^5/_{16}$"
(B)	102° (approx)	120° (approx)	4"r (approx)
(C)	2"r (approx)	2"r (approx)	$1^3/_4$"r (approx)
(D)	4"	4"	$3^1/_2$"

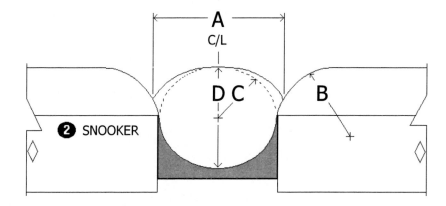

Figure 2-9 *Center pocket openings*

Corner Pocket

Rail 1 of Figure 2-10 represents the corner pocket of a pool table, and rail 2, a snooker table.

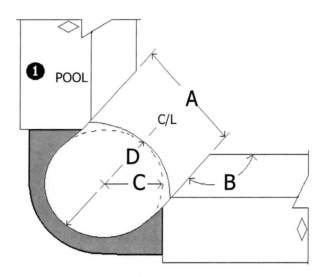

	Pool	Coin-operated	Snooker
(A)	$4^7/_8$" – $5^1/_8$"	5" - $5^1/_2$"	$3^3/_8$" - $3^5/_8$"
(B)	142° (approx)	150° (approx)	6"r (approx)
(C)	2"r (approx)	2"r (approx)	$1^3/_4$"r (approx)
(D)	4"	4"	$3^1/_2$"

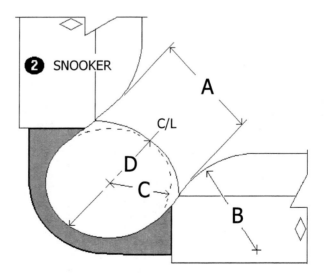

Figure 2-10 *Corner pocket openings*

Slate Pocket Cutout Dimensions

Although slate pocket cutouts should be 3½ to 4 inches in diameter, some manufacturers open them from 5 to 7 inches to allow pocket and hand clearance (Figure 2-11).

Once the table is assembled, however, the measurement from the interior edge of the slate cutout to the back of the pocket should be consistent with dimension D in Figures 2-9 and 2-10.

Corner and center pocket cutouts are usually cut using the same dimensions.

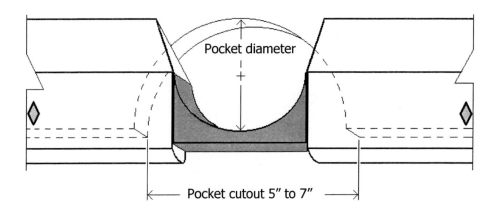

Figure 2-11 *Pocket cutouts*

MOLDED POCKETS, POCKET LINERS, AND GULLY BOOTS

Most molded pockets and pocket liners are made of plastic or rubber (Figure 2-12) and, on occasion, molded leather. Rubber seems to hold up better than plastic, and of course leather will outperform plastic and rubber. However, three or four sets of plastic pockets can be replaced at a cost less than one set of leather.

Pocket liners serve the same function as the top portion of the molded pocket. It trims the exposed raw wood of the rail and stapled rail cloth, and, simultaneously, directs the ball down into the pocket, or, with pocket liners, down onto the gully boot and ball return tracks. Generally, molded pockets and pocket liners come in one size and must be cut to fit individual tables.

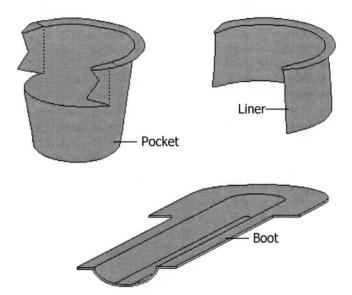

Figure 2-12 *Pocket, liner, boot*

Pocket boots are also plastic or rubber and are used with pocket liners. Their function is to quietly direct the ball to the ball return tracks. Often liners and boots are molded or otherwise assembled as one piece, but they still serve the same purpose (Figure 2-13).

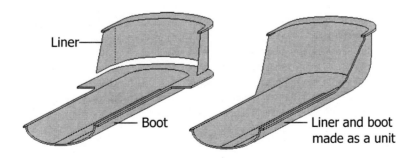

Figure 2-13 *Boot and liner*

GULLIES (BALL RETURNS)

A gully return is a system of tubes or tracks that returns all pocketed balls to a collection box at the end of the table, or to the side of most coin-operated tables. A variety of materials including wood, plastic and cardboard tubes, fiberglass, and plastic coated wire (Figure 2-14) are used for gully returns.

All gully systems have one inherent problem: trash. Napkins, cubes of chalk, pencils, tennis balls, stogies, children's toys, cue bumpers, light bulbs, ashtrays—anything that can fit into the pocket can plug it up. The debris can normally be fished out through the pocket or from beneath the table, but occasionally the table must be dismantled to get to it.

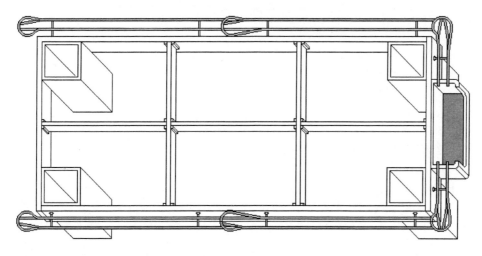

Figure 2-14 *Wire gully system*

PLAYING SURFACE

Playing surface is one of those phrases that can mean a couple of things. Often it refers to the bed or playing field of an assembled table; the actual area on which the game is played. But usually it simply refers to the underlying material the bed surface itself is made of.

Essentially, there are four (maybe five) kinds of underlying pool table playing surfaces: slate, marble, honeycomb, and particle board. Some outdoor pool table manufacturers are now using fiberglass or plastic composites to offer something that is weather resistant. I say this may be a fifth playing surface because some of the so-called composites are actually particle boards with a plastic or fiberglass coating. Let the buyer beware.

On The Level

I noticed a few years ago that most slate came from the United States, and manufacturers advertised "Genuine American Slate," like it was the best. Then they started importing it from Italy, and began advertising "Genuine Italian Slate," like that was the best. These days it is also imported from Belgium and China, and manufacturers are simply advertising "Genuine Slate."

"The best," then, cleanly comes from wherever you can get it.

SLATE

Slate is a gray, fine-grained, metamorphic rock that splits into natural slabs when mined. It is rigid, flat, not susceptible to warping, relatively inexpensive, and ideal for pool table beds. The majority of slate is quarried in Italy, Belgium, and

39

China where it is split, cut to size, and diamond honed flat. Often pocket cutouts and bolt holes are bored before the slate is crated and shipped. Because it is cheap and naturally abundant, slate is by far the best and most popular pool table playing surface.

Pool table slates are usually cut in one or three pieces (Figure 3-1). These sizes are typical but by no means are they a standard, a regulation, or a requirement, and some older tables even have two or four pieces, but that is rare.

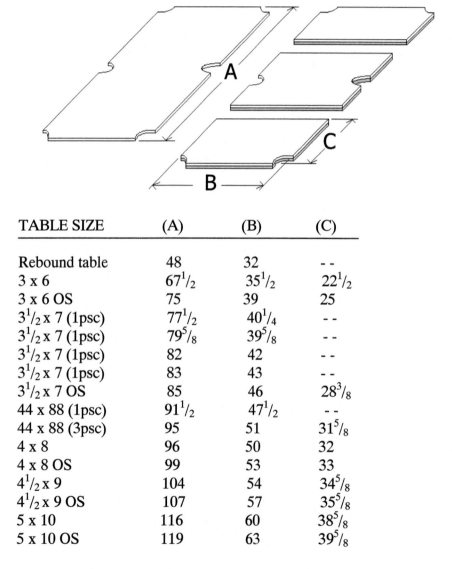

TABLE SIZE	(A)	(B)	(C)
Rebound table	48	32	- -
3 x 6	$67^1/_2$	$35^1/_2$	$22^1/_2$
3 x 6 OS	75	39	25
$3^1/_2$ x 7 (1psc)	$77^1/_2$	$40^1/_4$	- -
$3^1/_2$ x 7 (1psc)	$79^5/_8$	$39^5/_8$	- -
$3^1/_2$ x 7 (1psc)	82	42	- -
$3^1/_2$ x 7 (1psc)	83	43	- -
$3^1/_2$ x 7 OS	85	46	$28^3/_8$
44 x 88 (1psc)	$91^1/_2$	$47^1/_2$	- -
44 x 88 (3psc)	95	51	$31^5/_8$
4 x 8	96	50	32
4 x 8 OS	99	53	33
$4^1/_2$ x 9	104	54	$34^5/_8$
$4^1/_2$ x 9 OS	107	57	$35^5/_8$
5 x 10	116	60	$38^5/_8$
5 x 10 OS	119	63	$39^5/_8$

Figure 3-1 *Common slate sizes in inches*

Usually the length of each piece of slate in a set of three (dimension C in Figure 3-1) is the same for all three pieces of a matched set; however, in some rare cases a set of slates may have a center section that is longer than the ends. Even if this is the situation, the overall dimension (dimension A in Figure 3-1) should remain constant.

Slates are sized according to the way tables are designed. T-rails attach to the side of the slate. Because this was one of the original designs, the slate is considered "standard size." In order for flat rails to attach to the slate without changing the dimension of the playing field, the slate is extended beneath the rails. Therefore, this larger slate is designated "oversize." Other slates end just below the cushions, and the rails attach to the frame instead of the slate. This smaller slate is referred to as "undersize." Figure 3-2 illustrates the same playing field size using standard, oversize, and undersize slates.

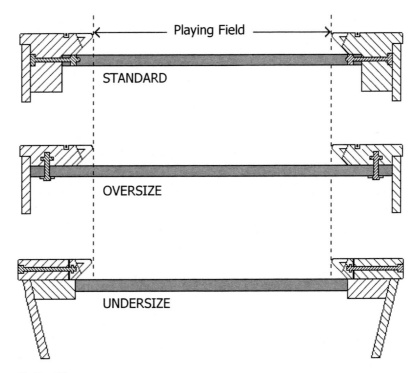

Figure 3-2 *Slate sizing*

If a table is constructed and assembled properly it makes little difference, from a levelness standpoint, whether or not the slate is one or more pieces. However, one-piece slates are generally undersize and, therefore, will not extend beneath the rails, so are not considered regulation by popular sanctioning boards. Some 7- and 8-foot tables have a one-piece slate bed and others have three pieces. However, because of weight, all 9-foot and larger tables have multiple slates.

Often each individual section of a three-piece slate set is backed with a $^3/_4$-inch thick tacking board. The tacking board is attached to the bottom perimeter of each slate to help prevent warping, and to allow a way to tack the bed cloth to the table. With unbacked slate the cloth must be attached to the frame or glued to the slate itself. Although some sanctioning boards require a tacking strip for regulation tables, neither system is better than the other because the tacking board backing doesn't always prevent warping.

Slates on most pool tables are $^3/_4$ to $1^1/_8$ inch thick. On occasion, an older table might have a $1^1/_4$ or $1^1/_2$ inch slate, but rarely would anything thicker be found. (A recent exception is Connelly's 2-inch "Ultima.") Once the cloth has been stapled to the tacking board, though, the slate appears to be $^3/_4$ of an inch thicker than it actually is, and that is probably the reason for stories of 2- and 3-inch thick slate tables. The two real advantages to thicker slate are a heavier, more stable table, which is less likely, and sometimes impossible, to be bumped around, and the slate is less likely to warp or crack. However, although thinner slate is more apt to warp or crack, it can happen to slate of any thickness.

In some cases, the seams of three-piece slate sets are dowelled and pined to keep the pieces flush to each other, and then honed to make a matched set. This provides an extremely accurate means of leveling (Figure 3-3).

Because of expense, however, the seams of most of today's three-piece slate sets are center screwed to the frame instead of dowelled (Figure 3-3), and are only as level as the frame, or the mechanics ability or willingness to properly shim them.

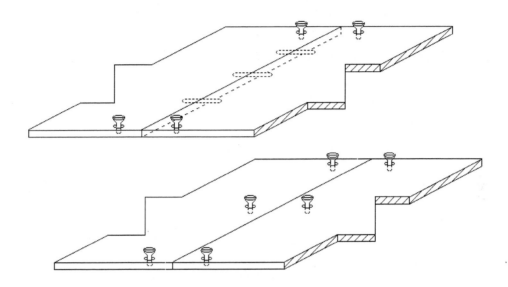

Figure 3-3 *Slates are dowelled or screwed*

Slate Screw and Rail Bolt Holes

Slate holes are drilled according to manufacturers' specifications, depending on how they want their slates and rails attached to a particular table frame.

However, there are usually eighteen rail bolt holes (three per rail) and sixteen slate screw holes. Rail bolt hole sizes vary between $1/2$" and $1^1/4$" in diameter for flat rails, and $5/16$" to $1/2$" for T-rails. Slate screw holes vary between $1/8$" and $3/8$" in diameter.

The distance between holes also depend on the manufacturer, but they range between 10 to 18 inches for rail bolts, and slate screw holes depend on the location of the frame members (Figure 3-4).

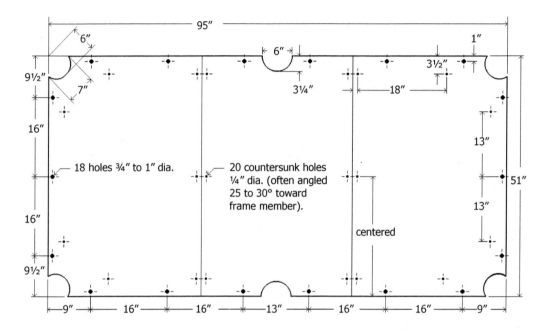

Figure 3-4 *Typical drill pattern for 51 x 95" three-piece slate set*

MARBLE

Marble, like slate, is a metamorphic rock that has been successfully used for pool table beds for years. Marble is flat, true, and has substantial weight. It is, however, more brittle than slate, and, consequently, more susceptible to cracking or breaking.

HONEYCOMB

Honeycomb beds are made with 5- or 6-inch wide strips of corrugated cardboard (like cardboard boxes) laid on edge, in a honeycomb fashion. The cardboard is then sandwiched between two thin sheets (usually $^1/_4$ to $^3/_8$ inch) of particle board to make a 5- or 6-inch thick bed. These beds usually stay relatively level as long as they do not get wet. However, they are light, and susceptible to being bumped and moved as a player shoots.

On The Level

Some years ago there was a table bed called "Slateen," and now one called "Slatron," and one more called "Permaslate." Although they sound like they could be some high-tech man-made slate, they are simply particle board or fiberboard, some even painted slate-gray. They should be avoided.

PARTICLE BOARD

A particle board bed is simply a sheet of particle board, usually $^3/_4$ inch thick (but could be up to 2 inches), set in the table to take the place of slate. It is a cheap and ineffective means to manufacture a table. Particle board tables wobble, warp, chip, ding, and sound cheap.

COMPOSITE

Composite beds are relatively expensive when they are 2-inch sheets of molded fiberglass or plastic and cut to pool table dimensions. However, some plastic or fiberglass covered particle board or fiber board playing surfaces are called composites.

PLAYING FIELD

Except in special cases, like those used for a physically disabled person, pool tables have a playing field height of between

28 and 30 inches, although BCA regulation is $29^1/_4$ inches, plus or minus $^1/_4$ inch.

Three reasons for height variations:

1. Not all tables are built to meet any standards.

2. When resting on thick carpet, a table could sink as much as half an inch.

3. If installed on a floor with a pitch, like a garage or basement, one side or end of a table could be shimmed an inch or more to make it level.

Table height is measured from the floor to the top of the playing field, not to the top of the rails (Figure 3-5).

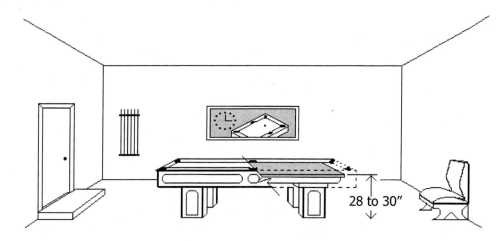

Figure 3-5 *Standard height of playing surface*

The overall width and length of different types of pool tables vary depending on the width of their rails. However, the playing field should be the same for any given table size.

The playing field is measured from cushion tip (nose) to cushion tip. For example, the playing dimensions for a full-size 4 x 8 table, whether it has narrow or wide rails should measure 46 inches wide by 92 inches long (4 x 8 is roughly the slate size). Playing field dimensions for the most common tables are listed in Figure 3-6.

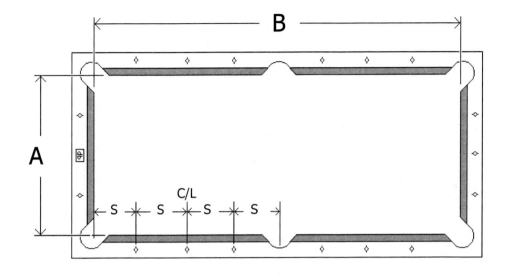

	3 x 6	$3^1/_2$ x 7	44 x 88	4 x 8	$4^1/_2$ x 9	5 x 10	6 x 12
(A)	36	40	44	46	50	56	70
(B)	72	80	88	92	100	112	140
(S)	9	10	11	$11^1/_2$	$12^1/_2$	14	$17^1/_2$

Figure 3-6 *Common playing field dimensions*

Sights

Sight spacing is determined by table size. The middle sight is placed in the center of the rail, and the other two are centered between the middle sight and the center of the pockets or edge of the playing field. For example, the four spaces between the sights of a 44 x 88 table equal 44 inches (11 x 4 = 44). Common sight spacing is shown as (S) in Figure 3-6.

Some manufacturers don't realize the significance of the relationship between the sights and the playing field, so botch their locations, but a good bank player certainly understands their relevance. If you want to know how sights are used to make banking easy without worrying about the Diamond System, see *A Rookie's Guide to Playing Winning Pool*, at rookie-guide.com or phoenix**billiards**.com.

PLAYING FIELD LAYOUTS

Although the following figures depict the different table layouts of spots and strings, most are only referred to and not actually drawn on the playing field; a pool table, for instance, will usually have only a foot spot.

Trick of the Trade

If desired, string lines and spots can be drawn on the playing field with either a carbon pencil or a felt-tip marker.

Spots are normally pre-manufactured and attached to the playing field with pre-applied adhesive, but can be drawn on with a pencil or felt-tip pen.

Pool Table Layout

The long string is an imaginary line that divides the width of the playing field in half. It aligns with the center sights of the head and foot rails (Figure 3-7).

The center string line divides the length of the playing field in half. It should align with the center of each center pocket.

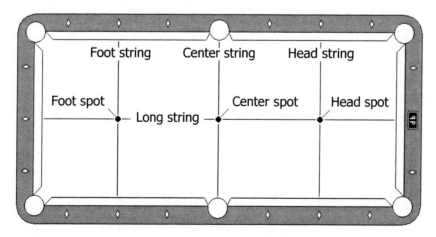

Figure 3-7 *Pool table spot and string locations*

Head and foot strings quarter the length of the playing field, and aligns with the center sights of their respective side rails.

The head, center, and foot spots are located where the head, center, and foot strings intersect with the long string.

Trick of the Trade

Although a head spot is not necessary on a pool table, if marked, it can be used to easily locate the head string, or to allow the choice of breaking from either end to increase the life of the billiard cloth.

The area between the head rail and the head string is the area of balk (also known as the kitchen); this is where the cue ball is placed when a foul occurs, or during the initial break.

The foot spot is the point at which the apex of the triangle of balls is racked. Generally, only the foot spot is marked, and string lines are not.

Snooker Table Layout

The long, foot, and center strings for a snooker table are imaginary lines that are found in the same manner as those on a pool table. The head string, however, has a specific dimension from the head rail, which does not necessarily quarter that end of the table (dimension F in Figure 3-8). Head, center, and foot spots are located at the intersection of the string lines. All spots are marked, but string lines are not.

Within the D-ring is the area of balk; this is where the cue ball is placed when a foul occurs, or during the initial break. The D-ring should always be marked on the table.

The foot spot is the point at which the apex of the triangle of red balls is racked.

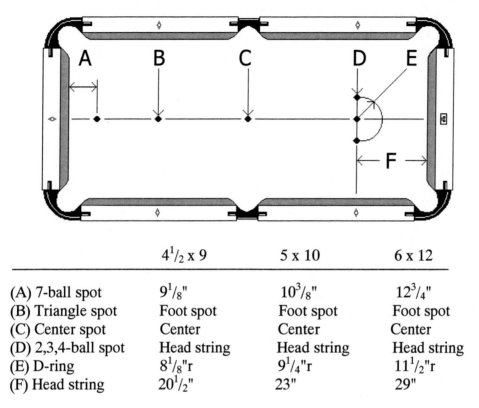

	$4^1/_2$ x 9	5 x 10	6 x 12
(A) 7-ball spot	$9^1/_8$"	$10^3/_8$"	$12^3/_4$"
(B) Triangle spot	Foot spot	Foot spot	Foot spot
(C) Center spot	Center	Center	Center
(D) 2,3,4-ball spot	Head string	Head string	Head string
(E) D-ring	$8^1/_8$"r	$9^1/_4$"r	$11^1/_2$"r
(F) Head string	$20^1/_2$"	23"	29"

Figure 3-8 *Snooker layout*

Trick of the Trade

You can use a piece of string and two carbon pencils can make a compass. Use one pencil as the pivot, and the other to draw the semicircle. However, a template made from some stiff material like pasteboard, Masonite, or thin plywood is the easiest and surest way to draw a D-ring.

A snooker table also has a 7-ball spot at the foot of the table, and a 2-ball and a 3-ball spot where the head string intersects the arc of the D-ring. The relative positions of these spots, and size of the D-ring, change somewhat depending on the size of the table. Their positions are listed in Figure 3-8.

If your table size is not listed, use these handy formulas.

A = .091 x length of playing field.

B = .5 x width of playing field.

E = .164 x width of playing field.

F = .207 x length of playing field.

Carom Table Layout

The head, foot, and center strings for a carom table are imaginary lines that are found in the same manner as those on a pool table. Head, center, and foot spots are located at the intersection of the string lines. All spots are marked, but string lines are usually not (Figure 3-9).

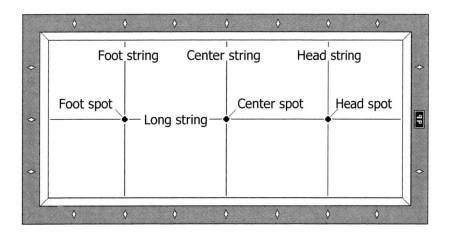

Figure 3-9 *Carom layout*

Bumper Pool Layout

Balls are aligned two on each side of the opposite color pocket hole with the marked ball in front of the pocket hole, and spots should be placed at each of these points (Figure 3-10).

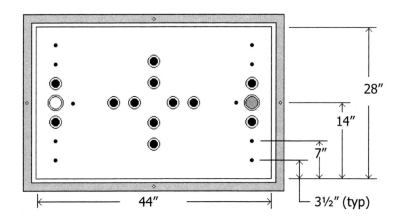

Figure 3-10 *Bumper pool layout*

WORDS OF EXPERIENCE

Although its size is not godly, Camelback Mountain pushes out of the "Valley of The Sun" like the hump of a camel, lording over the vastness of the cities below. I can stand on the hump, at the summit, pivot three hundred and sixty degrees and take in the panoramic vista of downtown Phoenix to the southwest, Glendale and Peoria to the west, Cave Creek and Carefree to the north, Superstition Mountain and Apache Junction to the east, Mesa and Tempe to the South, and Paradise Valley and Scottsdale beneath me.

The climb from Echo Canyon takes roughly an hour, and is strenuous. Still, for me, the view is well worth the effort. From there, I can see the valley in which I now work. From one end to the other, a hundred miles in every direction, I can see it in one sweeping motion. I crisscross this enormous arroyo every day in pursuit of the thousands of pool tables down there.

I have traveled from Barry Goldwater's nine-foot antique exposed frame table, with hand carved aprons, legs, and pockets sitting in the Wrigley Mansion, to a rancher's more common board and slat frame table sitting in a bunkhouse in Queen Creek. I have traveled from the hundreds of classic tables in mobile home parks around Apache Junction, to a retiree's unicabinet, unirail table in Sun City. I have traveled from a thousand standard and nonstandard tables in residences and apartment complexes, to a hundred coin-operated bar tables. I have worked on them all.

It's an awesome feeling.

CABINETS AND FRAMES

Pool table frames are as varied as are table manufacturers, but fall into two general categories. One is a table in which the cabinet is also the frame; the exposed portion of the table supplies the support for the slate and table. The second category has a hidden frame; the exposed portions are decorative and supply no, or very little, support.

Within the first category of the cabinet supporting the table, there are three styles: classic, tapered, and box. The hidden frame category also has three styles: boxed-beam, beam and slat, and board. The names given here to the various styles of cabinets and frames simply reflect their appearance, or the manner in which they were constructed.

CABINETS

Cabinet tables are those in which the exposed portion of the table supplies the support for the plating surface and table.

Classic Cabinet

The classic cabinet can be found virtually anywhere in the world, and has not changed much, if any, in hundreds of years. The cabinet is built on four or six legs with supporting members bolted between them making a rectangular table (Figure 4-1).

Even though this classic style has been around as long as pool tables have been in use, it has one basic design flaw. Because the legs are placed at the extreme ends of the frame, over time the weight of the slate forces the center to sag, in some cases as much as half an inch or more. Some manufacturers remedied the problem by introducing six-legged tables, but they are more expensive and as much trouble to level as is a sagging frame. Figure 5-1 depicts a typical six-legged table.

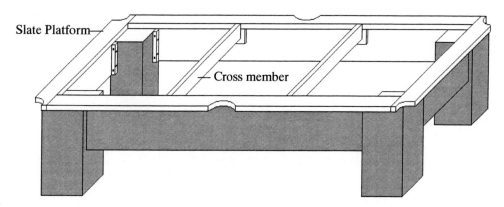

Figure 4-1 *Classic four-legged cabinet*

Tapered Cabinet

Another exposed table is the tapered cabinet, so named because of its shape. This style is usually built as a pre-assembled unicabinet that tapers inward toward the bottom, but it can also be assembled components that are attached at the corners with metal brackets or wood blocks (Figure 4-2). Also, the slate platform on some of these tables varies in construction quality from cheap $^3/_4$-inch, three-ply plywood or fiberboard, to a substantial 2-inch hardwood.

These tables come with a variety of leg shapes, cylindrical, Queen-Ann, ball and claw, lion's paw, tapered, etc. Also, the cabinet can be cut with scrollwork, cambers, and routed designs, but it is still a basic taper style cabinet. Most modern tables are of this design.

Considering strength versus lightness, the tapered cabinet is probably one of the best-designed cabinet, if lightness is indeed a plus. It does, however, have a propensity to warp cater cornered causing the table to wobble corner to corner, often making leveling difficult. Also, some tapered cabinet tables have undersize slate, which means the rails are attached to the cabinet or frame, as opposed to oversize slates where the rails attach to the slate.

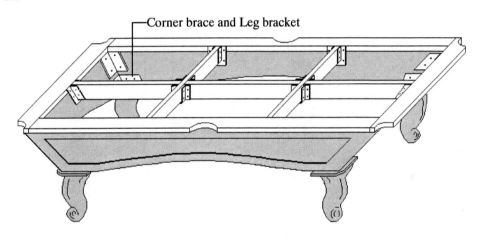

Corner brace and Leg bracket

Figure 4-2 *Tapered style cabinet*

Box Cabinet

The box cabinet is also a pre-assembled unicabinet and it too can taper inward toward the bottom, but not always. It differs from the tapered cabinet in that the top rails are contained within the cabinet or as part of the cabinet.

Box cabinets are durable, made to take excessive abuse, and with the right equipment are easier to transport and install than most. Consequently, most coin-operated tables are this style (Figure 4-3).

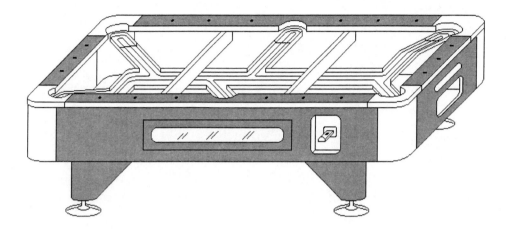

Figure 4-3 *Box style frame*

HIDDEN FRAMES

The other category of cabinets and frames is the hidden frame; the exposed portions of the cabinet are cover-ups or blinds, which produce no support for the tables.

Boxed-beam

The massive beams of a boxed-beam frame make it the heaviest style frame built (Figure 4-4). The most famous of this type frame is the Brunswick Gold Crown, with L shaped poplar beams. However, the beams could be steel, glue-laminated, or some other such material. The long side beams extend the length of the frame and are bolted together with end beams. The center of the frame is a grid-work of cross members for added strength and durability.

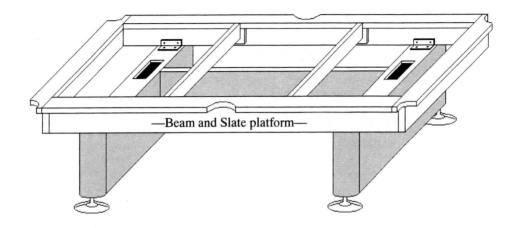

Figure 4-4 *Boxed-beam frame*

Beam and Slat Frame

The beam and slat frame consists of two or three beams that run the length of the frame with three or five slats bridging them (Figure 4-5). The slats of these tables can be 1 x 6's, 1 x 8's, 2 x 4's, or any such material. Unbacked slate, particle board, or some other playing surface is laid directly onto the slats, which double as slate tacking boards. These frames are usually made from inferior materials, and are found on less expensive home-style tables.

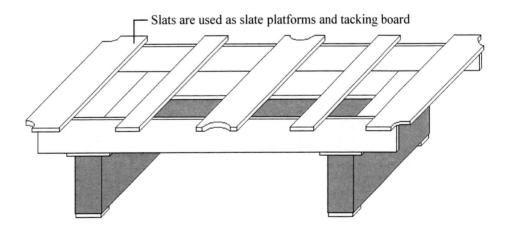

Figure 4-5 *Beam and Slat frame*

Board Frame

The board frame is also found on home-style tables. It is simply 1 x 8 inch (or such) boards, usually plywood or particle board, set on edge and bolted together to form a rectangular structure (Figure 4-6). Cross boards are added to make a fairly rigid frame that can support its thin, unbacked slate or particle board playing surface quite effectively.

$3/4$-inch frame boards double as slate platform

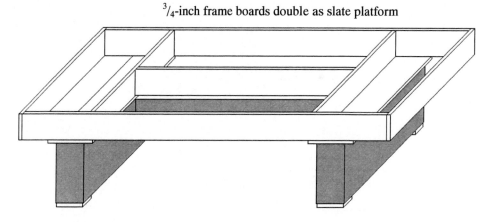

Figure 4-6 *Board frame*

LEGS AND PEDESTALS

Pool table cabinets and frames are supported by one of two means: legs or pedestals. Other than aesthetics, there is no apparent advantage or disadvantage to one or the other when they are well constructed. Both have been around for years, and have always looked and worked fine.

The pedestal table is often considered second-rate. That attitude comes from the fact that pedestals support most inexpensive tables. However, there are some fine tables manufactured with pedestals. The Brunswick Gold Crown is an excellent example. Beneath its substantial frame are two pedestals that are properly set for correct weight distribution, and are connected by a substantial stretcher beam. The frame never bows or sags.

LEGS

If a table has four or six individual supports, it is said to have legs. Legs can be square (Figure 5-1), rectangular, cylindrical, Queen-Ann, tapered, or whatever, as long as they are individually attached to the table.

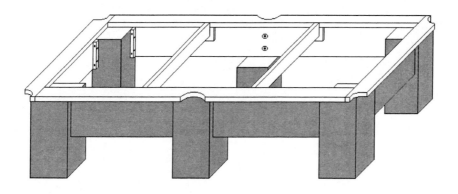

Figure 5-1 *Six-legged table frame*

PEDESTALS

Pedestal supports are usually two rectangular boxes, one at each end of the table, extending the width of the frame. Properly set toward the center of the table to accept the weight distribution evenly, pedestal supports rarely let the frame sag. Also, having a stretcher beam spanning between the two supports helps to reduce frame sag and end-to-end wobble (Figure 5-2).

Contemporary tables can have some version of a single center support that would be considered a pedestal, but they usually are not very stable.

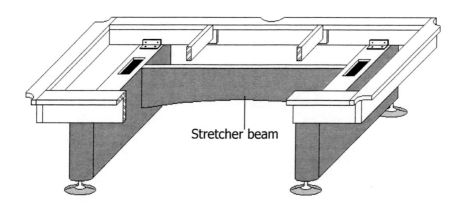

Stretcher beam

Figure 5-2 *Pedestals with stretcher beam*

BILLIARD CLOTH

No matter what anyone calls it in normal conversation, billiard cloth is not felt. Felt is a matted fabric of wool or hair or fur fibers adhered together by heat, moisture, and pressure. Billiard cloth is a woven material, either 100 percent worsted wool or a blend of nylon and wool at a ratio of 20 or 25 percent nylon, and 80 or 75 percent wool. The cloth weight is between 17 and 22 ounces per square foot, with 21/22 ounce being the accepted standard.

On The Level

I once re-covered a coin-operated table that had previously been covered with felt purchased from a fabric store. The felt had been glued onto the surface of the entire slate and rails.
What a mess!

Most billiard cloth comes in linear yards in varying widths, from 62 inches for standard cloth to 78 inches for worsted, smooth-nap cloth. The nap will be either directional or non-directional. Directional cloth is so named because the nap lies in one direction. Non-directional cloth has nap that lies in random directions. Some cloth has a rubber or canvas backing material bonded to its underside.

Billiard cloth is available in more than forty colors and blends. Most colors are included in Table 6-1.

AVOCADO	CHARCOAL	GRAPE	PEWTER
AZTEC	COPPER	GREEN	PURPLE
BANKERS GRAY	CORAL	KHAKI	RED
BLACK	DARK GREEN	LAVENDER	ROSE
BLUE	DENVER BLUE	MAHOGANY	RUST
BLUE GREEN	EGGPLANT	MAUVE	SEA FOAM
BROWN	ELECTRIC BLUE	MUSTARD	SPRUCE
BURGUNDY	ENGLISH	OLIVE	SURF
CAMEL	EVERGREEN	ORANGE	TAUPE
CANADIAN	GOLD	PAPRIKA	TEAL

Table 6-1 *Common cloth colors*

Cloth colors are constantly being changed and updated to stay in step with modern home decor. Also available are a few multicolored designer cloth made by weaving together different colored threads.

Furthermore, as if more than forty colors are not enough, tables can be covered in two-tone combinations; that is, the cushions one color and the bed cloth another. Some possible combinations: red bed with navy cushions, copper bed with camel cushions, black bed with gray cushions, navy bed with electric blue cushions, mauve bed with surf cushions (very southwestern). Combinations for sport's colors, like purple and orange for the Phoenix Suns basketball team, or navy and gray for the Dallas Cowboys football team, for example, are also possible. Of course, these colors can be reversed, and the combinations are limited only by imagination and taste.

Also, some companies are selling sports logos, flags, family pictures, etc. that are inked onto the cloth. These can look fantastic or gross, depending on your decorating abilities, but the inked area leaves the cloth slick and hard to play on.

11

Disassemble

All pool tables should be dismantled before they are moved, transported, or stored. Ruining a set of rails, aprons, or legs is entirely too easy when trying to pick up a table by parts that were not designed to carry the weight of the complete table.

Dismantling a table is not a difficult task. It is simply a matter of starting at the top and removing components until reaching the bottom. Also, if it is to be put back together in some reasonable approximation of its former self, it must be dismantled with care and purpose.

Do not leave function and location of parts to memory. To be on the safe side, mark everything, including all nuts, bolts, and screws. As time passes, it becomes difficult to recall how all the pieces fit if they are not marked.

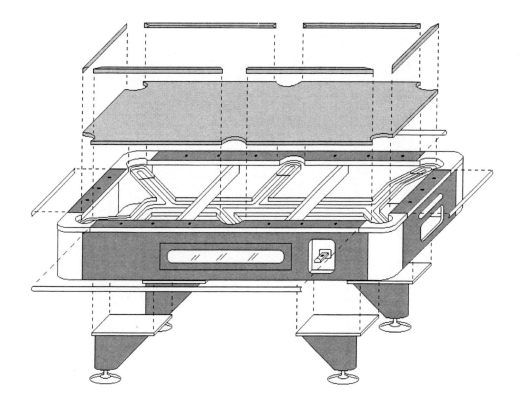

Exploded view of coin-operated table

IN THIS SECTION

ONE-PIECE SLATE TABLES

DISASSEMBLE

Coin-operated and similar one-piece slate pool tables are the simplest in regards to dismantling, yet they are the most abused. Although most companies that move tables as a profession will not bother disassembling these and many other one-piece slate tables, to do so is much easier, safer, and far less damaging to the table. It is especially less damaging if a novice is doing the work without proper dollies or advice.

Virtually all coin-operated tables are dismantled by first removing the trim from the outside edge of the top rail. This trim covers the rail bolts (or screws) that hold the detachable rails to the rail assembly. Once these bolts are removed, the rails will fall away (Figure 7-1).

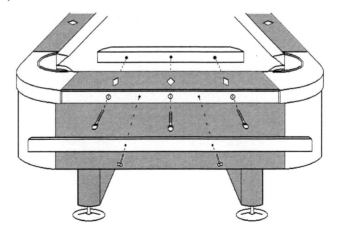

Figure 7-1 *Coin-operated table*

65

Location of Rails

The relative location of each rail should be marked even though some rails are interchangeable. Thus, when it comes time to reinstall them, they can be returned to their original position to insure proper fit. It doesn't really matter what marking system is used as long as the stationary part of the rail and the detachable part are marked to correspond to each other. A standard system is to mark the head rail #1, then, clockwise around the table, the rails are marked #2, #3, #4, #5, and #6. Interchangeable rails are #1 and #4, #2 and #5, and #3 and #6 (Figure 7-2).

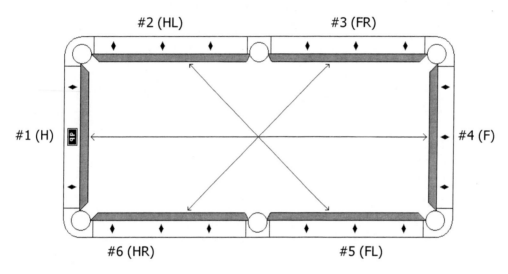

Figure 7-2 *Interchangeable rails*

Another system used by some manufacturers is to mark the head rail H, the rail to the right of the head HR, and the rail to the left HL. The foot of the table is marked F, the rail to the right FR, and the rail to the lift FL (Figure 7-2). Notice that the head and foot rails are interchangeable. So are the rails marked left (HL, FL), as are the rails marked right (HR, FR).

Just because some rails can be interchanged, it is not always a good idea to do so because rail bolt holes don't always align properly, causing an improper fit and poor ball rebound.

Remove Slate

After removing the rails, the slate can be lifted straight up and out of the table frame. This process only takes two people if each person stands at opposite ends of the table and places a hand in each of the corner pocket cutouts of the slate, and lifts from there. If the slate is in good shape, it will not warp, bend, crack, or break when only its corners are used to lift it. In fact, this is the easiest way to carry it.

Normally the bed cloth of a one-piece slate or coin-operated table is glued to the slate and will not have to be removed unless it is to be replaced.

If the table is to be stored or moved to another location, simply set the slate, with the bed cloth still attached, on its long edge and lean it against a solid object, like a wall.

The cabinet of a coin-operated slate table is usually constructed as a unicabinet, and, except for the legs, cannot be dismantled further.

Caution

After the table has been turned onto its side, remove the top legs first. This keeps the table from becoming top heavy and tipping over, and it prevents someone from banging his or her head by suddenly raising up into the top protruding legs.

Remove Legs

The easiest way to remove the legs, **whether the table has been dismantled or not**, is to turn the table onto its side. First, though, notice which side *does not* have the ball door or coin mechanism; the table should lie on that side. Before it is rolled over, though, remove the adjustable levelers (foot pods) from that side of the table to prevent damage to them. Next, simply roll the table over the legs without levelers and onto its side, directly onto a four-wheel dolly.

The last step is to unbolt the legs (Figure 7-3). The table is ready to be transported to storage or its new location. Reverse the above instructions to assemble coin-operated and other one-piece slate tables.

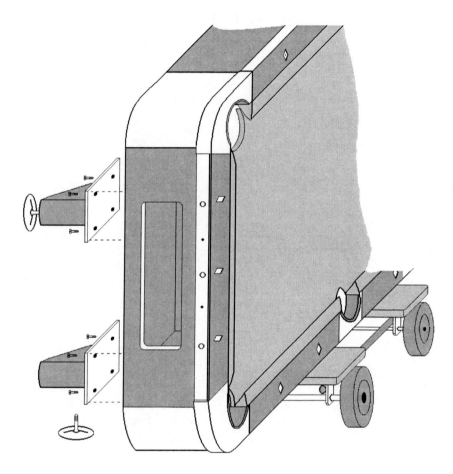

Figure 7-3 *Remove legs*

THREE-PIECE SLATE TABLES

Included in the three-piece slate table category are nearly all T-rail and flat rail tables. The exception is that one-piece slate tables also have flat rails, and, although rare, some three-piece slates are found on coin-operated (detachable rail) tables.

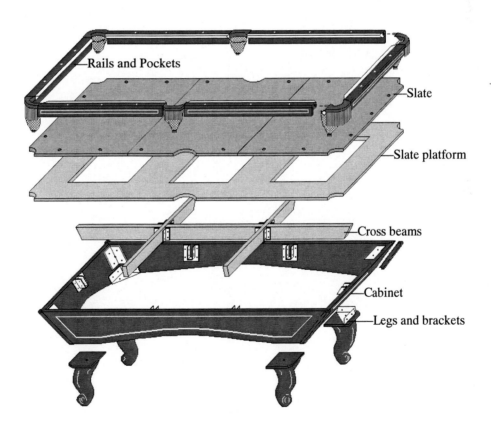

Figure 8-1 *Three-piece slate table (Asian)*

69

POCKETS

When dismantling three-piece slate tables, it is always easier to start with the pockets.

Molded Pockets

Molded pockets (leather, rubber, plastic), or pocket liners should be removed first. Molded pockets and liners are held in place with screws, nails, or staples (Figure 8-2).

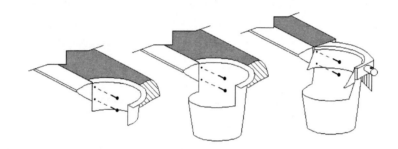

Figure 8-2 *Remove nails or staples*

Using a tack puller or small screwdriver, carefully remove whichever is there. If a nail or staple head should tear through the pocket, it may still be usable if it did not rip.

Tube gully returns that are friction held in place by the gully pockets will fall free once the pockets are removed.

Leather Pockets

The webbing of exposed leather pockets is fastened onto the slate tacking board or table frame, either beneath the slate (pocket 1 in Figure 8-3) or along the inside of the pocket cutout (pocket 2 in Figure 8-3). If possible, detach the webbing before the rails are removed. Again, use a tack puller or small screwdriver.

With some T-rail tables, the webbing might be covered with the bed cloth. In this case, detach the webbing after the rails and bed cloth are removed.

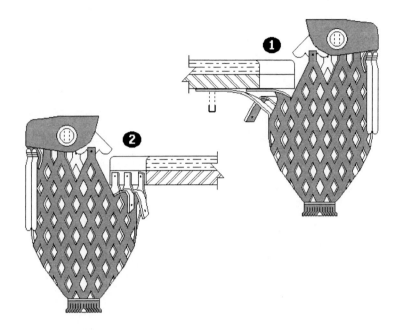

Figure 8-3 *Remove nails or staples*

APRONS

Aprons (often called blinds) are affixed to the top rail or table frame to hide the edge of the slate. Some aprons are permanently affixed to the rail (rail 1 in Figure 8-4), and some are detachable and often must be removed before unbolting the rails.

Flat rail aprons are attached to the rail by either exposed screws going through the apron and into the rail base (rail 2 in Figure 8-4), or hidden brackets or wood blocks at the back of the apron (rail 3 in Figure 8-4). Screws are also used to attach some T-rail aprons, but most have 4-inch pocket bolts that screw in from the bottom of the apron, holding the apron and pockets. Other T-rails have rosettes instead of aprons that cover the rail bolts (rail 4 in Figure 8-4).

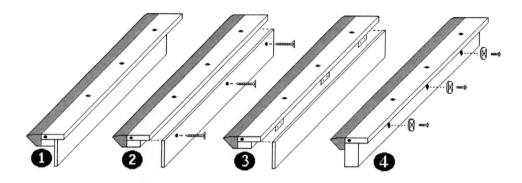

Figure 8-4 *Aprons or rosettes*

Aprons on tables with molded pockets or most gully return systems are fastened together at their ends with corners, castings, blocks, or caps (Figure 8-5).

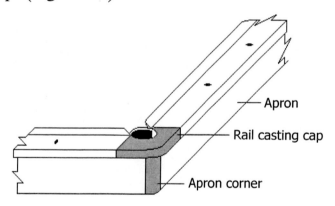

Figure 8-5 *Aprons with corners*

These aprons can be dismantled from beneath the table, or the whole rail assembly can be turned up side down then dismantled, see "Flat Rails With Mitered Corners or Castings" later in this chapter.

RAILS

Some rails are interchangeable; however, they should be reinstalled to their original position to insure proper fit. For an explanation on interchangeable rails and marking their position, refer to Chapter 7. Interchangeable rails are #1 and #4, #2 and #5, and #3 and #6 (Figure 8-6).

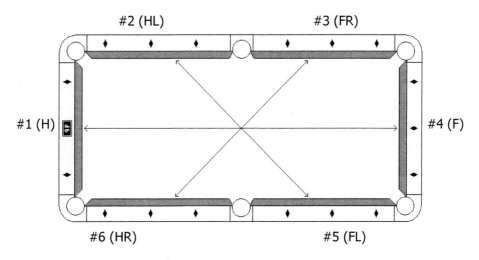

Figure 8-6 *Interchangeable rails*

T-Rails

T-rails are removed by first unscrewing the pocket bolts (Figure 8-7), and then the rail bolts.

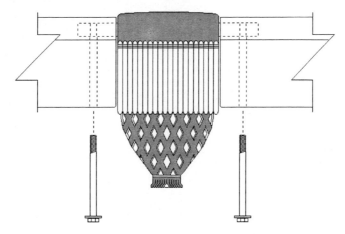

Figure 8-7 *Remove pocket bolts*

Also, T-rails are attached to the table by three to five rail bolts that penetrate the rail base and screw into lugs leaded into the slate (Figure 8-8).

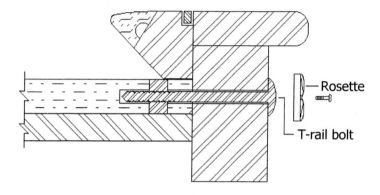

Figure 8-8 *T-rail bolts*

These T-rail bolts can be hex-head with standard threads, but most are a nonstandard, thrust-head style with two holes that accepts a two-prong type tool instead of a standard wrench or socket (Figure 8-9).

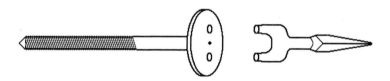

Figure 8-9 *Rail bolt tool*

Since T-rails hang on the sides of the table they may fall once the bolts have been removed, so they should be taken off one at a time and with care (Figure 8-10).

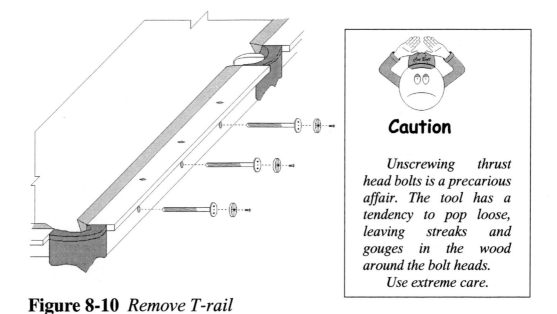

Caution

Unscrewing thrust head bolts is a precarious affair. The tool has a tendency to pop loose, leaving streaks and gouges in the wood around the bolt heads.
Use extreme care.

Figure 8-10 *Remove T-rail*

Flat Rails With Leather Pockets

Flat rails are fastened to the table with three or four bolts that come up through the slate or frame from beneath the table and usually fasten into lugs within the rail base (Figure 8-11).

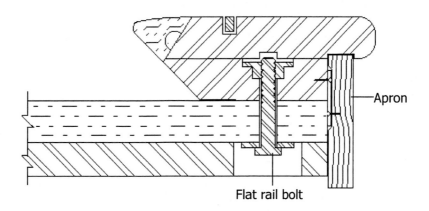

Figure 8-11 *Flat rail bolt*

It is rare to find a table with bolts going down through the flat rail and into the frame, but some are made that way. The bolt heads are covered with metal or plastic that act as rail sights. Also, Sears sold a table in which the rail screws are covered by the rail and are not visible. On these tables, the exposed feather strip must be removed before the rails can be taken off.

Leather pocket irons are bolted onto the rails from the bottom, and cannot usually be removed until the rails are unbolted from the slate. The normal procedure is to remove the rail bolts first (Figure 8-12).

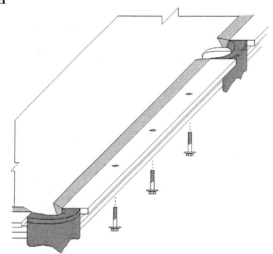

Figure 8-11 *Remove flat rail bolts*

Next, slide the rail assembly to one side exposing the pocket bolts past the edge of the slate or frame, then unbolt the pockets from beneath the table (Figure 8-13).

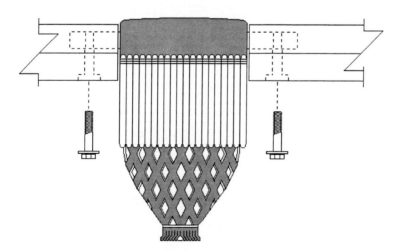

Figure 8-13 *Remove pocket bolts*

This works well and causes little problem as long as the rails are not allowed to fall from the table, as the pocket bolts are unscrewed.

However, leather pocket bolts are more accessible by unbolting one pocket bolt from each center pocket and separating the rails into two horseshoe assemblies (Figure 8-14).

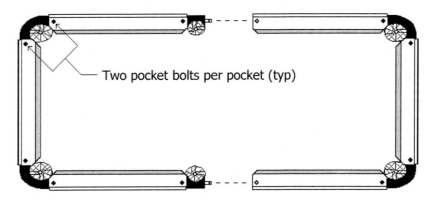

Two pocket bolts per pocket (typ)

Figure 8-14 *Rails upside down*

These assemblies can then be carefully turned upside down on the table. The pocket bolts can then be easily removed.

Flat Rails With Mitered Corners or Castings

Flat rails with mitered corners have plastic or metal castings or caps where the rails come together. These assemblies can be dismantled from beneath the table; taking off each part—aprons, castings, and rails—one at a time.

Caution

The points of attachment of the rails and pockets were not designed to handle the weight of the rails being turned over. Use two people and extreme care. Also, the rails should not be stored and transported in this configuration, or with the pockets still attached to any rail.

However, like the leather pocket assembly, it is often easier to turn the whole unit upside down on top of the table and dismantle it into manageable parts, from that position (Figure 8-15). This can be done by removing the eighteen to twenty-four rail bolts then, with one person on each end, simply turning the assembly over. Do not attempt to store or transport the rail assembly in this configuration. Dismantle it first.

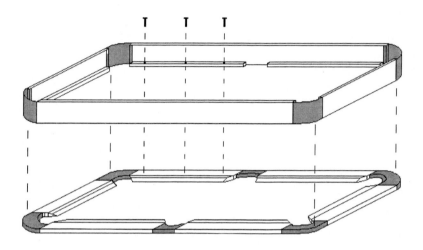

Figure 8-15 *Rails and aprons upside down*

Unirail Assembly

A unirail assembly is one in which all six flat rails are constructed as a unit, and cannot be further dismantled (Figure 8-16).

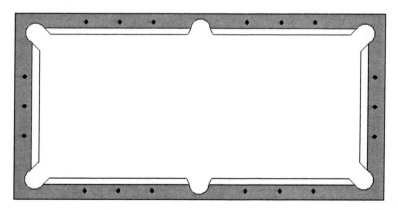

Figure 8-16 *Unirail assembly*

Remove all the rail bolts, and then lift the rail assembly up from the table. Aprons attached to the unit are usually disassembled first, but can often be removed by turning the whole assembly upside down, see Figure 8-14 above. Often, unirails are part of a box frame table with no removable aprons.

GULLIES

Gully return systems are generally not in the way and can be left attached to the frame. Some tube and board gullies, however, must be removed to uncover the rail bolts. Others are friction held by gully pockets and will fall free once the pockets are removed.

BED CLOTH

Bed cloth is either glued to the slate or stapled to the slate tacking board. Since cloth is only glued along the edges, it can easily be peeled loose. If the cloth is stapled, the staples must be removed carefully to salvage the cloth, unless it is to be replaced. New cloth is not always necessary just because the old cloth is removed for table disassembling. If the table is to be re-covered, refer to Chapters 17 and 18.

SLATE

Most three-piece slates are honed individually and during table manufacturing are selected on a first come first used basis. They are not matched to each other or to the table, and their location and orientation on the table can be changed at will.

In contrast, others are honed together, as matched sets, and superior slates are honed and pinned as matched sets (see Chapter 15). The position of matched slate sets should not be switched or changed in their relationship to each other.

If the slates are not pinned, it is often hard to tell which are matched and which are not. The safest procedure is to treat all slate sets as if they are matched. Mark the slates to indicate which is the head and which is the foot, and how the center slate lies in relation to the ends.

The simplest marking method is an arrow drawn with a felt pen or piece of chalk across one side (off center) of all three slates. With the arrowhead pointed toward the head of the table, there is no possible way to get the end slates confused (Figure 8-17). Some antique tables are marked with dimples on the side of the slate.

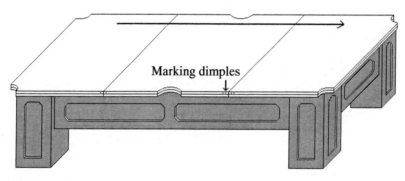

Figure 8-17 *Mark slates*

Three-piece slate sets are attached to the frame by slate screws (Figure 8-18).

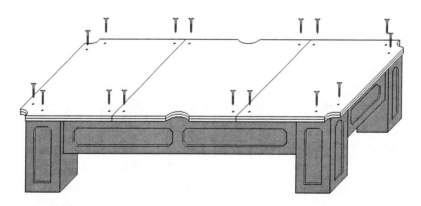

Figure 8-18 *Remove slate screws*

Slate screws are countersunk into the slate, and may be covered with bees' wax or hard putty. Wax can be scooped from the countersunk recesses with a common-end screwdriver. Hardened putty, though, must be chipped out with a small chisel or screwdriver. It is possible that small pieces of the slate will also chip away with the putty. These chipped areas are nothing to be overly concerned with since they can be filled when the slate screws are refilled. Some slates also have screws that hold the slate tacking board to the slate. Removing the tacking board screws is not necessary. These screws are only 1½ to 2 inches long, while the slate frame screws are 3 to 4 inches long.

After removing the slate screws, set the slates aside; lean them against a wall or some other solid object. If they are stacked flat on the floor, a couple boards should be put beneath the bottom slate so it can be lifted later. See Chapters 9 and 10 for crating, transporting, and storage.

CABINETS AND FRAMES

There are several kinds of table frames, and most can be disassembled into smaller, more manageable pieces,

Removing every part from the frame to obtain manageable pieces is not necessary. Judge how much the frame should be dismantled by its size, weight, and possibility of damage. Most frames are dismantled, in some form or another, by first removing any cross members, then separating the main frame members from their legs or pedestals. The classic cabinet, for example, separates at the legs, and it is usually only necessary to unbolt the side panels, leaving the legs attached to the end panels (Figure 8-19). The cross members may or may not be screwed to the side panels.

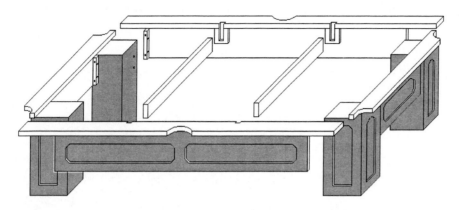

Figure 8-19 *Classic cabinet*

Boxed-beam, beam and slat, and board frames are separated from their legs or pedestals and either left together as a frame unit or can be dismantled further, depending on circumstance, table design, and space available (Figures 8-20, 8-21, and 8-22)

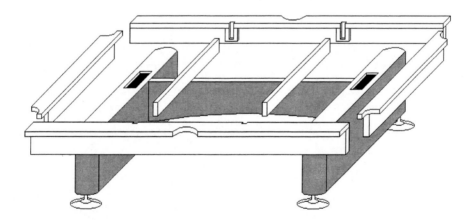

Figure 8-20 *Box-beam frame*

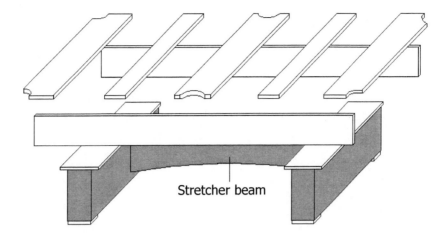

Figure 8-21 *Beam & slat frame*

Stretcher beams must also be separated from their pedestals. Don't attempt moving the pedestals and stretcher beam as a unit. The points of attachment are too weak and the potential damage is extreme.

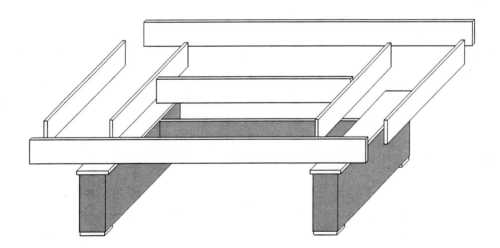

Figure 8-22 *Board frame*

Normally, only the legs or pedestals are detachable from uni-cabinets like the tapered cabinet in Figure 8-23.

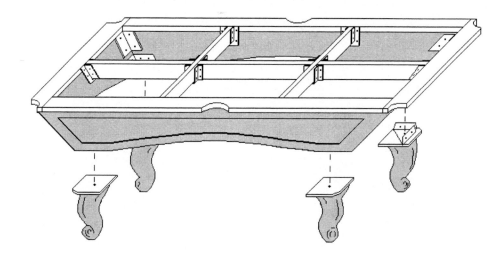

Figure 8-23 *Tapered cabinet*

All other frames are dismantled in some similar manner as above, and most legs are detached as shown in Figure 8-24.

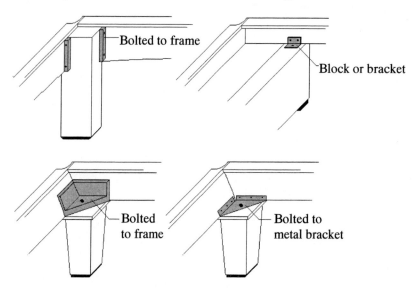

Figure 8-24 *Standard leg attachments*

Some tables have removable slate platforms, but usually they should be left attached to the frame. Once the frame has been dismantled, the table is ready to be transported, or stored. Mark all parts so they can be returned to their original position.

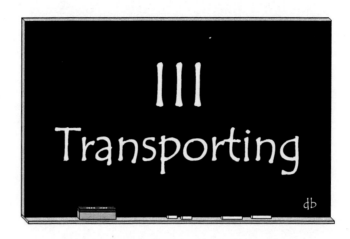

III
Transporting

Care must be taken when packing, crating, storing, and transporting any pool table, whether it is being moved from one room to another, across town, or traversing the country.

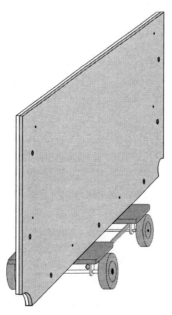

Use a dolly whenever possible.

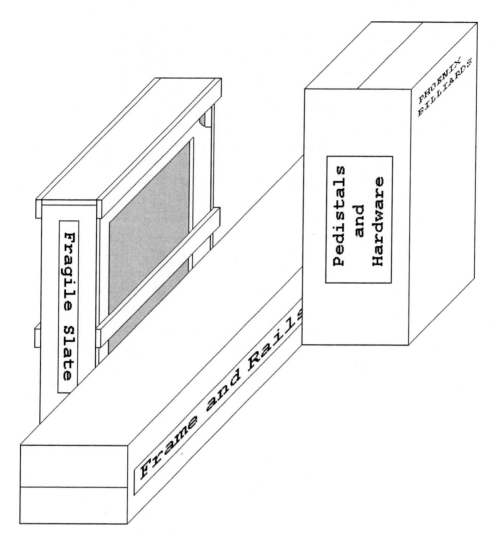

Complete table in three packages

IN THIS SECTION

PACKING AND CRATING

PACKING

Taking the time to carefully dismantle a pool table, and then damaging it during transporting or storage seems irrational. Any part of a table subject to scratching or damage should be wrapped separately from other parts. If the table is being transported a long distance or stored for more than a few days, all disassembled pieces like rails, pockets, corner caps, leg levelers, etc., should be wrapped and packed in cardboard boxes of some sort. Larger items such as long aprons and rails can be wrapped separately or taped together, face to face, to prevent scratching.

Bed cloth can usually be folded, but should be rolled around two or more pool cues to prevent creases and fold marks.

Unicabinets can be wrapped in shipping blankets like any other large piece of furniture.

All nuts, bolts, and screws should be packaged in small bags and marked to indicate what they are used for—rail bolts, pocket bolts, slate screws, etc.

CRATING

It's not always necessary to crate the slate, especially on short moves, but, to minimize the change of chipping, cracking, or breaking, it is almost unanimous among large moving companies that slates be crated before they will take on the responsibility of moving them.

Crating slates is downright simple. A few pieces of 1-inch by 4-inch lumber and some 6-penny nails or 2-inch construction (drywall) screws is all that is needed. Because of weight, three-piece slates should be crated individually. That means three crates, but they are easier to build than is moving all three slates in one large crate (Figure 9-1).

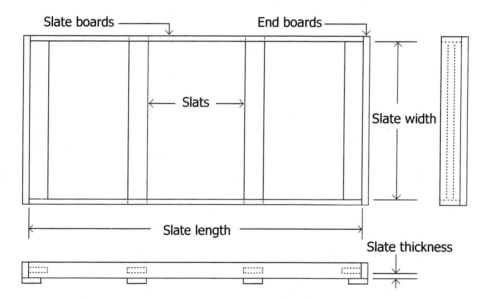

Figure 9-1 *Slate crate*

The interior dimension of the crate will be the same as the exterior dimension of the slate. Each crate is constructed using at least twelve boards (with large one-piece slates one or two extra slats can be added). The two longest side boards are cut the same length as the slate. The lengths of the four interior slats are cut the same as the width of the slate. The four exterior slats and two end boards are cut $1^1/_2$ inches longer than the width of the slate.

Construct the exterior frame of the crate first. This is done by nailing or screwing the ends of the end boards to the ends of the long side boards, making a rectangular frame. The long boards are mounted to the inside so the interior of the rectangle is the same size as the perimeter dimension of the slate. Attach the exterior slats, one on each end and the others spaced equally along one side of the rectangle, to complete a shell.

Lay the shell flat on the floor with the exterior slats down (Figure 9-2). Then, carefully, slide the slate into the shell.

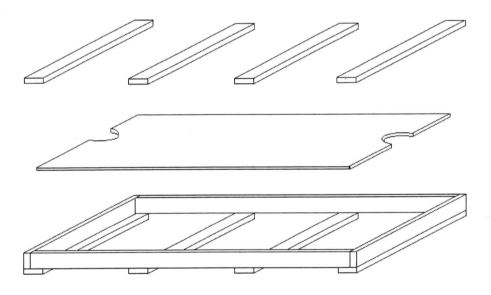

Figure 9-2 *Exploded crate*

Next, position two interior slats into the shell, one at each end, and snugly on top of the slate. The other slats are placed equidistant across the crate. Attach the interior slats through both the long side boards and the end boards. This type of crate is superior to all others because no matter how thick the slate is or whether or not it's backed, the crate is built to fit the thickness without shims or adjustments.

On The Level

I once walked off a job to dismantle and crate a table because the homeowner insisted that I work barefooted.

Sorry, but I refuse to carry two hundred pounds of slate on a slick floor in my stocking feet, not to mention running in and to build the crate.

A year or so later the same lady called me back to reassemble the table.

"I'd be happy to," I said. "But I still don't work in my stocking feet."

"Well, I'll get someone else."

"Please do . . ."

Figure 9-2 depicts a center slate of a three-piece slate set. End slates would be crated in a like manner.

The only difference between a crate for a one-piece slate and a three-piece slate is size. The one-piece slate crates are longer and wider. Also, wrapping the entire slate with packing paper or such material before it is placed into the crate should protect any bed cloth still attached to the one-piece slate. Do not, however, use corrugated cardboard (cardboard boxes) because the corrugation can transfer to the bed cloth, leaving it full of ripples.

MOVING AND STORAGE

As easy and quick as it might first appear, moving or transporting a pool table without first dismantling it is a mistake. This includes bar and other one-piece slate tables, although some are designed to be moved as a unit, and, in fact, are shipped from the factory that way. Most damage done to a table during shipping is done because the table was not disassembled (see Chapters 7 and 8). Pool tables are extremely top heavy. The frame and legs are not built for side loading, as would happen if a table were turned onto its side to be moved through a doorway, a hallway, etc. Nor are tables built to be lifted by their weakest points: rails, aprons, and slate screws. Damage caused by moving a table frequently costs more to repair than the cost of a professional mover, and certainly more than the time it would have taken had the table been dismantled correctly in the first place. Furthermore, once a table has been disassembled, packaged, and crated properly, it can be loaded and shipped anywhere with ease, and without worry.

Although recommended, packaging the accessories and crating the slate is not always necessary if the table is to be hauled only a short distance (for packaging and crating, see Chapter 9).

If packaging or crating is not used, special care must be taken to assure that the hardware, parts, and pieces are loaded safely and securely.

Slate can be individually hand carried, but, if possible, it should be wheeled standing on its edge on a mover's four-wheel dolly. It is also generally recommended that slate be trucked on its edge, tied securely to the front of the bed so it does not fall or shift. However, slate can be laid flat on the truck bed as long as it is not allowed to bounce or slide during transporting. Make sure the truck bed is clean; don't allow anything to get between it and the slate. Padding beneath the slate is not necessary either. Any object that makes the slate lie uneven stands a chance of breaking it.

On The Level

Dolly good.
Hernia Bad.

If laid flat, three-piece slates should be stacked, one on top of the other, and secured at the front of the truck bed. Nothing is needed between them. Padding on top, however, is a good idea to protect other table hardware.

All parts of the cabinet, rails, and legs, if they were not packed in cardboard containers, should be wrapped in moving blankets, and can be laid on top of, and around, the secured slate.

A table that is to be stored for a long period should be carefully packaged and marked. All packages and hardware should be stored in a tight group and away from any work area where they could be damaged. Slate, whether crated or not, should be stored on its edge (not flat), and in a dry, shaded spot.

Miscellaneous materials are the kind of paraphernalia needed to assemble a pool table but are not pool table components.

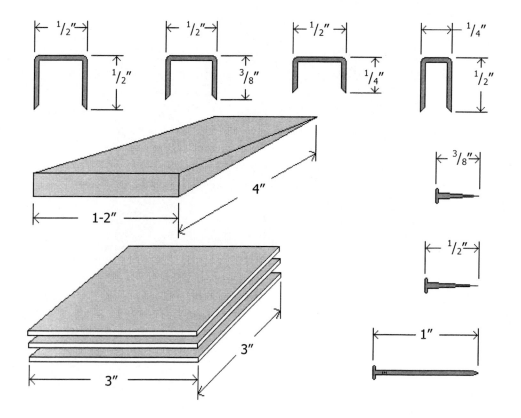

Staples, nails, tacks, wedges

IN THIS SECTION

Chapter 11. Miscellaneous Materials

MISCELLANEOUS MATERIALS

STAPLES

For ease of use alone, staples are the preferred method of attaching billiard cloth to a table. Any commercially available hand or electric stapler will work. A pneumatic upholsterer's stapler is nice, but not necessary.

The staple's crown width is unimportant, but is usually between $^1/_8$ and $^3/_8$ inches. The leg or penetration depth should be dictated by the job to be done. For billiard cloth, if the tacking wood is in good condition, use $^1/_4$ inch. In cases where the wood has deteriorated $^3/_8$ inch should be used. Longer staples are not needed for three reasons. First, because the cloth is stretched over the edge of the slate or rail, the pull on the staples is at right angles, and, therefore, $^1/_4$ inch will hold as well as anything longer. Second, longer staples tend to bend or break instead of seat, especially in hardwood and particle board, so they will not hold the cloth anyway. Third, when it comes time to remove the cloth for recovering, longer staples must be extracted one at a time, using a tack puller and pliers. Quarter inch staples, on the other hand, will easily pull free with the old cloth.

Staples used for leather pocket webbing at the bottom of the slate tacking board should be either $^3/_8$ or $^1/_2$ inch long to penetrate the thick leather and still hold the weight of the balls. Anything longer is extremely difficult to remove, and, more often than not, will simply bend anyway.

When tacking leather pocket webbing to the edge (as opposed to the bottom) of the tacking board use $^3/_4$ to 1 inch staples.

NAILS

Small nails are required for molded pockets and some leather pockets. Pocket nails should be between $^3/_4$ and 1 inch in length depending on the condition of the wood. Anything larger is unsightly, difficult to manage, and does unnecessary damage to the rails and tacking board.

Three-quarter inch nails or wood screws can be used on leather pocket webbing instead of staples.

TACKS

Carpet tacks are sometimes used instead of staples to secure cloth to the bed and rails of a table. At one time, they were the norm, and rarely were staples used. Staples are faster, easier, and do a superior job, however. Large carpet tacks can also be used to attach leather pockets, but they are also unsightly if exposed.

GLUE

There are two types of glue used in pool table maintenance and assemblage. One is a spray adhesive used for bed cloth. 3M brand 76, or 90 in hot areas such as garages, are excellent examples. The second glue is contact cement, which is used for cushions, cue tips, laminates, and often bed cloth.

SEAM FILLERS

Seam fillers are used to fill the countersunk screw holes in slate, and the seams of three-piece slate. Three kinds of fillers are commonly used. The least popular but very durable is auto body putty. Next is bees' wax, which is melted into the joint then smoothed over before it cools. And, because of its ease of use, the most popular seam filler is quick drying water putty, like Durham rock hard.

WEDGES

Wooden wedges are used chiefly to level the slate to the frame. Lone, thin, and wide (1-2" x 4") wedges are superior to short, thick, and narrow ones.

SHIMS

Shims can mean two things. They are wood wedges used chiefly to level the slate to the frame. Shims are also flat squares of material—wood, floor tiles, sheet rubber, etc.—that are inserted beneath pool table legs to level the frame.

TOOLS

Staple gun (hand or electric), rubber mallet, small hammer or tack hammer, Phillips screwdriver (electric power drive preferred), utility knife, putty knife, and ratchet and socket set.

Words of Experience

I have the local contract to deliver and assemble pool tables sold by a national consumer's club. The three pieces of slate of some tables are often shipped in a single crate. Shipping slate this way is okay for shippers who own and have the facility to operate fork lifts, but for most of us our only recourse is to take the slate out of the crate and haul them individually. This is fine as long as care is used.

On one such table a couple years ago, I broke down the crate and stacked the three pieces of slate in the back of my pickup, then loaded the rest of the table on top of the slate. On the way to the customer's house, I stopped at a red light that was on a fairly steep hill (yes, Phoenix has hills). When the light changed, I took off. The slate, of course, slid backward into the tailgate, which flew open. The slate hit the pavement scattering in a hundred pieces, and then the rest of the table landed on the pieces, and all skittered down the hill until coming to rest across both lanes of traffic. The young lady behind me screeched to a halt before crushing the table frame as it bumped her car. No damage was done to the car, the frame, or her. Lucky me.

A local dealer, and friend, Rick Spillman of the Billiard Store in Scottsdale, bailed me out. He had on hand a complete set of slate and hardware needed to restore the table, which I delivered that same afternoon.

Accidents can happen, and it helps to have friends in the business.

V
Installation

Installation of a pool table, including re-covering and replacing rail cushions, is often time-consuming and frustrating, but it is not difficult and can be enjoyable and satisfying if approached from a knowledgeable position.

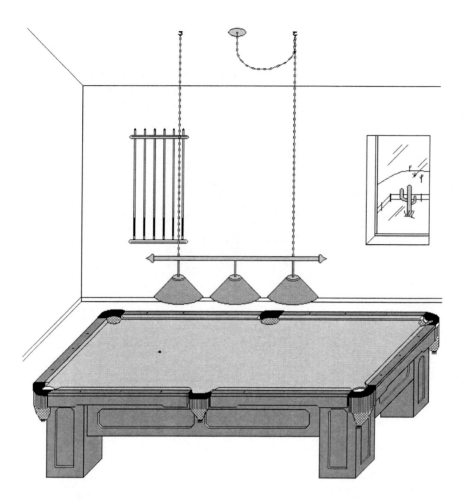

Arizona poolroom

IN THIS SECTION

POOL ROOM

Few homes are built with a pool table in mind; so finding a room of ideal size is rare. However, there are two ways to get around the size constrictions without poking holes in the drywall. One is a smaller table, and the other is a shorter cue.

DISTANCE FROM WALLS

Optimally, a room should be large enough to leave 5 feet along each side and each end of the table. A standard cue is 57 inches long, 3 inches shy of 5 feet, and, although some rails can be as wide as 8 inches, most are a narrow 4 to 6 inches (5-inch median). So, using 5 inches as a measuring guide allows 8 inches for stroking between the butt of the cue and the wall when the cue ball is at its worse position—frozen to a cushion—and the shot is perpendicular to the rail and wall. With 5 feet around the table, using a standard cue, there are no shots that cannot be made due to wall interference (Figure 12-1).

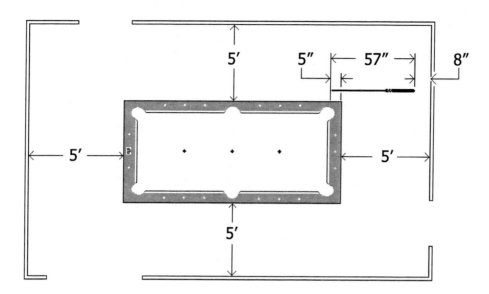

Figure 12-1 *Ideal table distance from a wall*

Normally, however, most shots are at an angle to the rail with the cue ball away from the cushion. Because of that, the clearances can be cut by 6 inches and allow minimal, but satisfactory, playing conditions. This 6-inch difference is per side and end, which is a decrease of a foot in overall room size. So $4^{1}/_{2}$ feet clearance per side and end is, if not ideal, quite playable using a standard cue.

On the Level

I once installed a table in a singlewide mobile home. There wasn't even enough room to walk around the table, let alone play. Can you imagine?

ROOM DIMENSION

Table 12-1 shows the optimum and minimum room dimensions for most pool table sizes.

STANDARD 57-INCH CUES

TABLE SIZE	OPTIMUM ROOM SIZE	MINIMUM ROOM SIZE
3 x 6	13' x 16'	12' x 15'
$3^1/_2$ x 7	13' 6" x 17'	12' 6" x 16'
44 x 88	13' 8" x 17' 8"	12' 8" x 16' 8"
4 x 8	14' x 18'	13' x 17'
$4^1/_2$ x 9	14' 6" x 19'	13' 6" x 18'
5 x 10	15' x 20'	14' x 19'
6 x 12	16' x 22'	15' x 21'

Table 12-1 *Room Dimensions*

A good rule-of-thumb for figuring the optimum room size is simply adding 10 feet to the table size. Accordingly, a 4 x 8 table needs a 14 x 18 room, and so forth. Subtract a foot overall to obtain the minimum room size. Or, if starting with the room, take its dimensions and subtract 10 feet. A 13 x 16 room, for example, will optimally accommodate a 3 x 6 table, and a 3 $^1/_2$ x 7 minimally.

Room dimensions can also be cut substantially by using a shorter cue, and figuring the distance from the wall as the same as the cue length. For example, using a 54-inch cue, instead of a standard 57-inch as in Table 12-1, a playable room size can successfully be decreased to 54 inches around the table.

A 48-inch cue will decrease the room size to 48 inches around the table. Using this criterion, then—if you want to split hairs—the optimum distance for a standard 57-inch cue can be 57 inches, instead of the recommended 5 feet.

Because there are no regulations that require a 57-inch cue, a cue can be cut to any length. Shorter than 48 inches, however, the cue becomes too cumbersome for good control.

To figure the room size using a shorter cue, double the cue length and add the overall table size. A 3 x 6 table using 48-inch (4 feet) cues, for example, can be set up in a room that is 11 x 14 (3' + 4' + 4' = 11') and (6' + 4' + 4' = 14').

Table 12-2 shows the room dimensions for 54-, 52-, and 48-inch cues.

NONSTANDARD CUES

TABLE SIZE	54" CUE ROOM SIZE	52" CUE ROOM SIZE	48" CUE ROOM SIZE
3 x 6	12' x 15'	11' 8" x 14' 8"	11' x 14'
3$\frac{1}{2}$ x 7	12' 6" x 16'	12' 2" x 15' 8"	11' 6" x 15'
44 x 88	12' 8" x 16' 4"	12' 4" x 16'	11' 8" x 15'4"
4 x 8	13' x 17'	12' 8" x 16' 8"	12' x 16'
4$\frac{1}{2}$ x 9	13' 6" x 18'	13' 2" x 17' 8"	12' 6" x 17'
5 x 10	14' x 19'	13' 8" x 18' 9"	13' x 18'
6 x 12	15' x 21'	14' 8" x 20' 8"	14' x 20'

Table 12-2 *Room Dimensions using cue lengths*

On the Level

I was invited to play on a table with so much junk under it I couldn't see from one side to the other. And stink! Mildew and dog markings (pool table legs are a dog's favorite spot) were so strong I couldn't concentrate on the game. Talk about home table advantage!

FOOT CLEARANCE

The floor beneath and around the pool table also needs to be clear of obstacles such as ledges, steps, benches, chairs, boxes, camping gear, toys, Rottweiler, etc. This clearance should be a minimum of 4 feet from the outer edge of the pool table (Figure 12-2). If clearance is not provided, a proper cuing stance cannot be obtained. Tripping over, kicking, and stepping around floor obstructions and furniture detracts greatly from the playability of the table and concentration on the game. Also, using the area beneath the table for storage, however convenient, can be an obstruction, not to mention tacky.

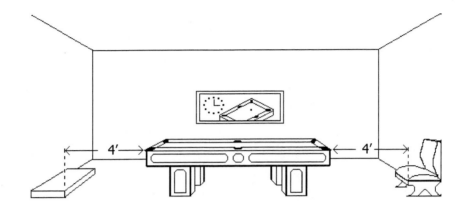

Table 12-2 *Distance from obstacles*

FLOORS AND CEILINGS

There is no recommended flooring material or ceiling height for a poolroom. A pool table can be leveled on any kind of floor—tile, wood, carpet—it doesn't matter. Some installers use carpet as an excuse for sloppy work, but the truth is any table can be leveled on any carpet, and carpet has the advantage of being quieter than other flooring. Uneven tiles like saltillo are as easy to level on as is concrete and smooth tiles. Upstairs rooms, however, tend to settle from the weight of a pool table, so the table should be re-leveled every month or so until settling stops.

A throw rug under a pool table will also soften the noise of balls rolling, when the table is on a tile floor; however, a rug on carpet does little for noise and tends to wrinkle around the legs, causing an irritating obstruction.

Although there is no recommended ceiling height, it really should be over eight feet. Anything lower can actually get in the way of the cues, and will get perforated by the cue tips.

LIGHT FIXTURES

Traditional pool table lights hang above the table, are supported from the ceiling by chains or cords, and come in many shapes and sizes.

Hanging lights are usually decorative, and add ambience to the poolroom. Fixtures with two or more incandescent lamps are superior to a single lamp simply because they distribute light more evenly across the table. However, whether one lamp or more, incandescent lights tend to cast distracting darkish shadows of the balls, cue, and player's hand.

Although some unavoidable light shadowing might still exist, good fluorescent lights eliminate most of the bothering shadows. Fluorescent fixtures that hang, though, are long and boxy, and not very attractive. But those that are attached directly to or recessed into the ceiling (although adding nothing to ambience) create a room that is bright, pleasant, and virtually shadow less.

There are no set rules on the height of a hanging light above the playing surface of a pool table, but eye level is usually acceptable. A good rule-of-thumb, though, since eye level varies with each person, is to place the lower rim of the fixture about 3 feet above the table (Figure 12-3), or $5^1/_2$ feet from the floor. It is also a good idea to have the bottom edge of the fixture slightly below eye level so it is low enough to prevent eyestrain, yet high enough to be out of the way of play.

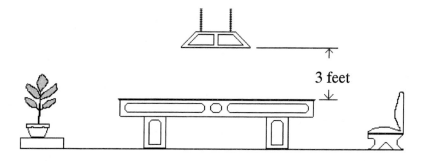

Figure 12-3 *Height above table*

UNCRATING

ONE-PIECE SLATE TABLES

Coin-operated and similar one-piece slate pool tables are the simplest in regards to uncrating and assembling. If new, most companies ship the tables pretty much assembled, in one box. The only tasks to do in this case is to remove the table from the box, set it on its side (preferably on a dolly) and attach the legs (Figure 13-1), then roll it upright. If the one-piece slate table was dismantled and not crated, refer to chapter 7, and simply reverse the disassembly instruction to assemble it.

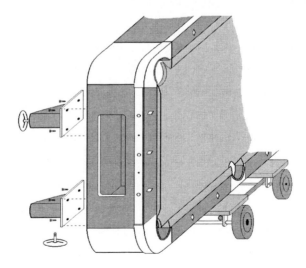

Figure 13-1 *Attach legs*

THREE-PIECE SLATE TABLES

Often, new tables will come in two crates or packages: cabinet/frame with all components—legs, rails, pockets, etc.—in one, and the slate in the other. Usually, though, each component will have its own crate or package making as many as six or seven, including the slate and rails, which are not show in Figure 13-2.

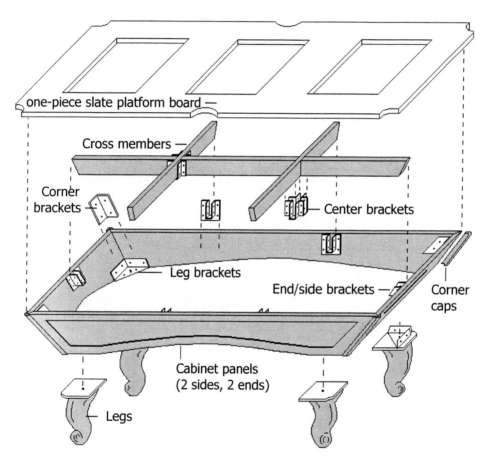

Figure 13-2 *Cabinet components*

Excluding the slate, carefully open each package and remove its contents. Following, I have listed the five most common packages and their contents. In parentheses, I have given the most common sizes. Although they may vary somewhat from model to model, their sizes will be close to those listed. An asterisk (*)

indicates an item that may be substituted for another item.

(1) In the hardware box there will be:
   18 rail bolts and washers ($^5/_{16}$" x 2")
   12 slate screws (1" to 3")
   12 leg screws ($1^1/_2$" construction screws)
   4 leg nuts—or bolts—and washers ($^5/_{16}$", 3" bolts)
   12 pocket bolts and washers ($^3/_8$" x 1")
   *A coil of rubber feather strips ($^1/_4$" x $^1/_4$" x 16')

Lay all hardware out in individual groups according to size and type. These groups should be laid along a wall or some other location away from where the out table is to be assembled.

(2) If the cabinet needs to be assembled, you will need the following components (this list will differ slightly depending on table brand, model, and cabinet style you have, and sizes are approximate):
   2 cabinet side panels (7' x 18")
   2 cabinet end panels (3' x 18")
   4 cabinet corner caps (2" x 18")
   5 cross member beams (2" x 4")
   6 end/side mounting brackets
   2 center brackets
   4 legs
   *4 corner brackets and 4 leg brackets, or
   4 combined leg / corner mounting brackets
   48 to 96 cabinet screws—or bolts ($^1/_4$" x $^3/_4$")
   Slate board (one-piece or 4 to 6 individual pieces)

Lay these on the floor in roughly their assembled position.

(3)   In the rail box there will be:
     2 end rails
     2 right side rails
     2 left side rails
     *6 wooden or plastic feather strips
Set the rail box aside for now.

(4)   The pocket box will contain:
     6 leather pockets
     *12 webbing screws
Set the pocket box aside for now.

(5)   The slate will be created individually or all three in one crate (Figure 13-3). The slate can be removed from the crate before the cabinet is assembled or after. I usually wait for the cabinet so I can take the slates directly to it.

Although slates can be broken, it takes a pretty good jolt. So, handle them with care, but do not be nervous about moving them, either. And use a dolly. Depending on the table brand and model, the slates may or may not have a slate backing board glued to them.

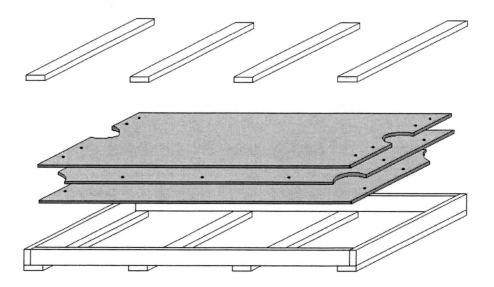

Figure 13-3 *Three pieces of unbacked slate.*

FRAMES AND CABINETS

If the table to be assembled is new, all parts and hardware will be packaged and labeled, and an instruction sheet or pamphlet will be provided. Contrary to a natural impulse to do otherwise, it is a good idea to (at least) look the instructions over to become familiar with the layout of the table.

Usually, tables that have been disassembled are easier to assemble than are new tables, straight from the box. If the table was dismantled properly, all pieces should be marked or labeled, and should fit.

On the Level

Some new tables are so poorly constructed that parts don't fit, and bolts and bolt holes don't line up. How sad!

If no markings or instructions are available, look over all parts, hardware, and components—rails, frame boards, aprons, pockets, legs, screws, nuts, bolts, nails, etc.—to become familiar with them. Then each part should be laid out in a group according to type and size. These groups should be set along a wall away from the area where the table is to be assembled. This is especially important if the table is

111

a used table with no labeling, markings, or instructions. With the hardware and components arranged in logical groups, under-standing the way they go together and their function is much easier.

ASSEMBLE

Pre-assembled Cabinet

Some cabinets are pre-assembled while others are not. With pre-assembled cabinets, "assembly" simply means to attach the legs to the cabinet or frame; the rest of the cabinet will already be together.

Assemble Cabinet

With cabinets that need to be assembled, all components and hardware—rails, cabinet panels, cross members, aprons, pockets, legs, screws, nuts, bolts, nails, etc.—will be packaged and labeled. Look them over to become familiar with them; by visualizing the way they go together and their function will make assembling much easier.

Occasionally the legs or pedestals themselves must be assembled before they can be attached to the cabinet. This is rare, but, if so, assemble them first.

Assemble the panels first, then add the cross members, the legs, and the slate platform last.

The cabinet panels are attached at each corner with wooden blocks (cabinet 1 in Figure 14-1), wooden braces with a gusset (cabinet 2 in Figure 14-1), metal corner and leg braces (cabinet 3 in Figure 14-1), or a metal corner and leg bracket combination (cabinet 4 in Figure 14-1).

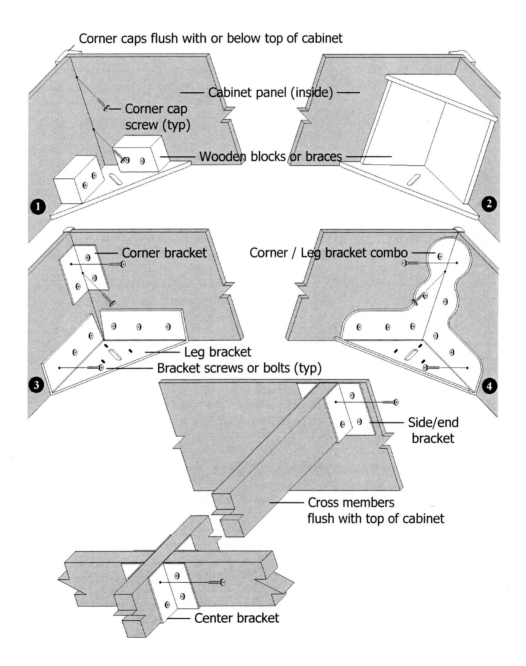

Figure 14-1 *Four different designs of brackets and braces*

All cabinets will have some variation of the four corner bracket or brace designs depicted in Figure 14-1. Whichever you have, make sure each part of the top of the cabinet (the part the slate or slate platform will rest on) is flush with each other (Figure 14-2). The corner caps should be flush or below the cabinet, but the bottom of the leg brackets *must* be flush with the cabinet's bottom. This is critical in the leveling procedure; if the cabinet or frame members are not flush there will be no easy or practical way to get the cabinet and slates level.

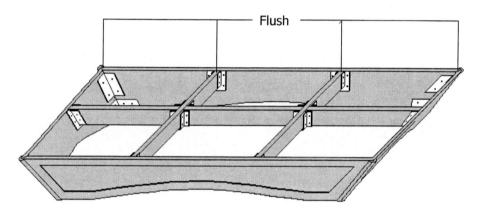

Figure 14-2 *Keep cabinet panels flush*

Square the cabinet

To square the cabinet, measure it diagonally in both directions. These two measurements should be as equal as possible (plus or minus $1/2$ inch) for the cabinet to be square (Figure 14-3).

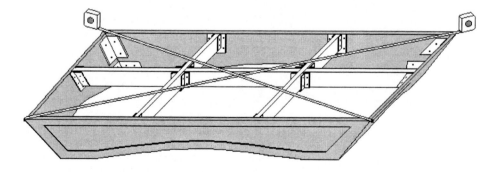

Figure 14-3 *Square cabinet*

Install Legs

The legs depicted in Figure 14-4 represent rams head legs. Square, tapered, or some other ornate or carved legs like Queen Anne, ball and claw, and so forth are installed the same.

Often, it is easier to turn the frame upside down to affix the legs, and then turn the whole assemblage right side up. With most, though, the frame must be set on the legs and fastened from above. Do whichever looks the easiest. Also, when the frame is turned right side up, do not allow any lateral force or weight onto the legs. If possible, rotate the frame in the air and set it down on all legs simultaneously.

As shown in Figure 14-1, some tables have separate leg supports and corner attachments and some are combined as a one – piece unit. These supports and attachments can be wood or metal brackets, depending on the table; however, the supports are usually assembled on the cabinet as it is put together so that only the legs need to be attached at this time, as shown in Figure 14-4. The exploded view in Figure 14-5 is provided for clarification only.

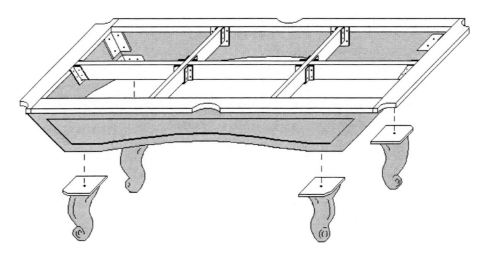

Figure 14-4 *Install legs to assembled cabinet*

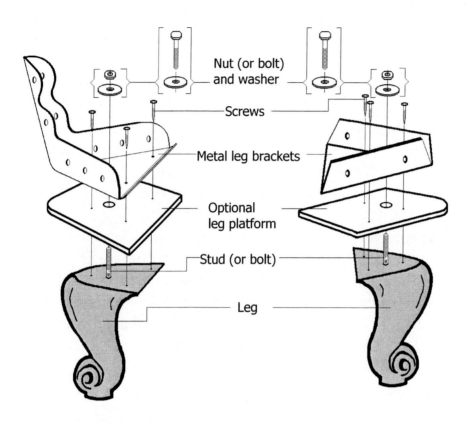

Nut (or bolt) and washer

Screws

Metal leg brackets

Optional leg platform

Stud (or bolt)

Leg

Figure 14-5 *Exploded detail of leg assembly*

As you install the legs, visually check and align each leg; make sure it is not too far back, too far forward, or twisted left or right; the legs should look like they are part of the table, not some afterthought. Tighten the center bolt or nut and then add the three leg screws to prevent the leg from twisting or turning.

Slate platforms

On some tables with **backed** slate, the slate platform is narrow and does not extend to the width and length of the slate (Figure 14-6), and is used as a slate-mounting surface only. Also, on tables with **unbacked** slate where there is only a narrow slate platform, the cloth must be glued onto the slate (see Chapter 17).

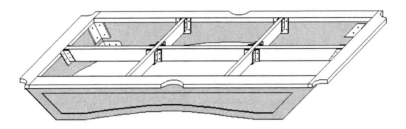

Figure 14-6 *Narrow slate platform*

Other tables with **unbacked** slate use a wide slate platform for both a platform and something to staple the bed cloth to (Figure 14-7). These slate platforms are as wide and long as the slates. Depending on the brand and model, slate platforms can be one, four, six, or even eight pieces.

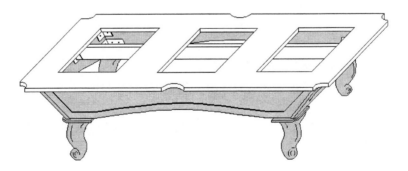

Figure 14-7 *Wide slate platform*

The slate platform board (or boards) should be centered on the cabinet with an equal amount of overhang around the table.

Assemble Frames

Usually the frame is assembled first. Leave all nuts, bolts, and screws loose until the entire frame is together, and then tighten. As the tightening process is being done, make sure each part of the top of the frame (the part the slate will set on) is flush with each of the other frame parts (Figure 14-8). This is critical in the leveling procedure; if the frame isn't flush there will be no easy or practical way to get the slates level.

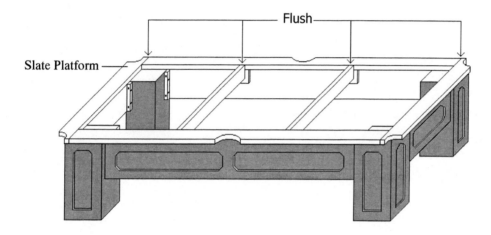

Figure 14-8 *Keep frame boards flush*

The legs on the table depicted in Figure 14-8 are assembled with the frame, and indeed, the legs are part of the frame. On some tables, like the box-beam frame (Figure 14-9), the legs or pedestals are separate and will need to be attached after the frame has been assembled.

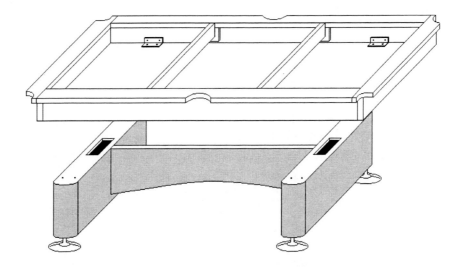

Figure 14-9 Box-beam frame with pedestals

Occasionally the legs or pedestals themselves must be assembled before they can be attached to the frame. If so, assembling them first or at the same time can be appropriate.

All other frames are assembled in some similar manner as above, and most legs are attached as shown in Figure 14-10.

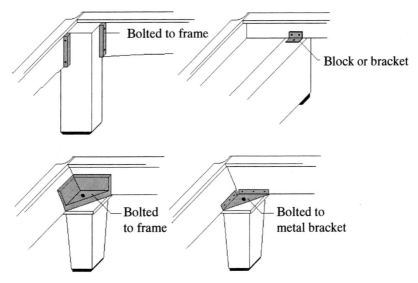

Figure 14-10 *Standard leg attachments*

The legs depicted in Figure 14-10 are square. Ornate or carved legs, like Queen Anne, ball and claw, and so forth are attached the same.

Often, it is easier to turn the frame upside down to affix the legs, and then turn the whole assemblage right side up. With some tables, though, the frame must be set on the legs and fastened from above. Do whichever looks the easiest, but, as the legs are attached, make sure the tops of them are flush or below the top of the frame. Most table legs cannot be assembled wrong, but some—especially cheap home style tables—can, and to repeat, if the legs protrude above the frame, the slates will rest on the top of them instead of the frame, making leveling almost impossible.

Also, when the frame is turned right side up, do not allow any lateral force or weight onto the legs. If possible, rotate the frame in the air and set it down on all legs simultaneously. If the table has screw-in levelers (round pods on the bottom of each leg) make sure they are screwed all the way in (up) so the frame will be at its lowest position.

To square the frame, measure it diagonally in both directions. These two measurements must be equal (within $\frac{1}{2}$ inch) for the frame to be square (Figure 14-11).

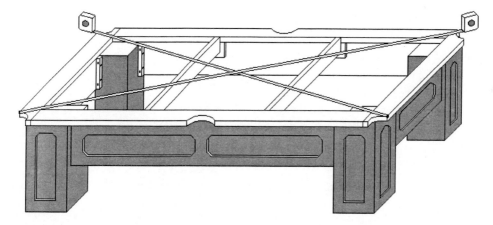

Figure 14-11 *Square frame*

TABLE POSITION

Once the cabinet or frame are assembled and squared, position the assemblage in the room where it is to stay. Determine which end of the table will be the foot and which will be the head. Often they are marked, but if no markings exist, chances are, from the table's standpoint, it does not matter. From the room's standpoint, though, it makes a difference. If the table is going to have a ball return system, the ball-return end is the foot: the foot is the end where the balls will be racked when playing. That end should be placed away from windows, doors, mirrors, cabinets, and so forth. When a ball leaves the table, it is usually during the break, flying off the foot end of the table.

In Chapter 12, Tables 12-1 and 12-2 give the proper distance the edge of a table should be from a wall. However, because the cabinet or frame is seldom as long or wide as the completed table, at this point in the assembly it is important to measure from the centerlines of the table, instead of the edge. Once the table has been assembled, it can be repositioned an inch or two to obtain the dimensions dictated in Chapter 12, if needed. To find the centerlines of the frame, simply determine its overall length and width, and divide each by two.

If the table is to be centered beneath a light or light fixture, measure from two adjacent walls to the center of the light plate (where the light attaches to the ceiling), or the center of the fixture itself if it is already in place. Use those distances to set the centerline of the table (Figure 14-12). That should be intuitive and logical, of course. But you never know!

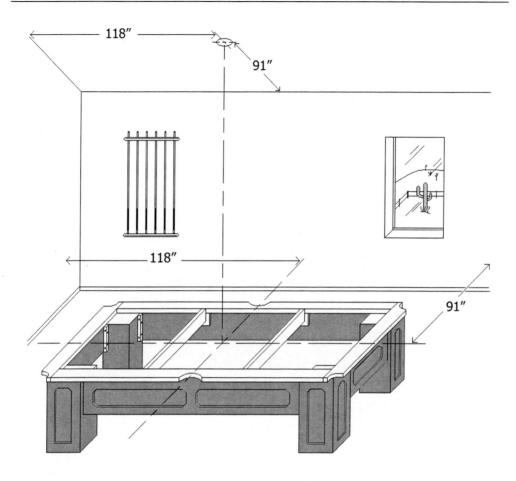

Figure 14-12 *9-foot table centered with light fixture*

Also, if the table is to be positioned in the middle of the room simply put the center of the cabinet or frame in the center of the room, then square it with the longest wall—still intuitive and logical.

If, however, the table is to be offset to one side or end of the room, the centerlines of the table should be positioned the proper distance from the closest wall or walls.

Although logical, this is where it is not so intuitive. Since the center of the pool table is now being used, knowing the overall assembled size of the table is important. If the overall size is not provided with the manufacturer's instructions, refer to Table 14-1 for an estimated overall size.

TABLE SIZE (in feet)	ESTIMATED OVERALL SIZE (narrow - in inches)	ESTIMATED OVERALL SIZE (wide - in inches)
3 x 6	44 x 78	46 x80
3^1/$_2$ x 7	50 x 90	52 x 92
Coin-op	--	53 x 93
44" x 88"	54 x 98	60 x 104
4 x 8	56 x 102	62 x 108
4^1/$_2$ x 9	60 x 110	66 x 116
5 x 10	66 x 122	72 x 128

Table 14-1 *Overall size of tables*

Divide the overall size by two to find the distance to the center from the outside edges of the assembled table, and then add that to the distance the table will sit from the wall.

For example, if the table is 4 x 8 with narrow rails, the overall length is 102 inches (from Table 14-1). Its optimum position from the wall is 60 inches (54 inches minimum, or a predetermined cue length, see Chapter 12, Tables 12-1 and 12-2). In this example, then, the distance from the wall to the center of the length of the table would be 111 inches [60 + (^{1}/$_2$ of 102) = 111].

Similarly, the width distance can be figured. The optimum distance from the wall is 60 inches; the overall width of the 4 x 8 table is 56 inches. Therefore, the centerline of the width of the table should be 88 inches from the wall [60 + ($^1/_2$ of 56) = 88] (Figure 14-13). After the table is assembled, it will be 5 feet from the two nearest walls.

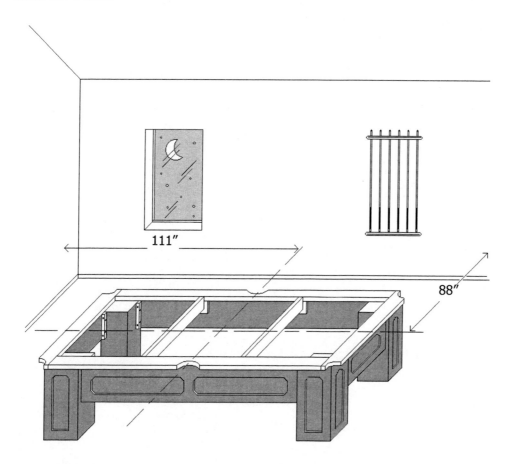

Figure 14-13 *Centerline distance to the walls for an 8-foot table*

PRE-LEVEL

Once positioned, the cabinet or frame should be leveled before adding the weight of the slate.

To begin, check the cabinet or frame from end-to-end to determine the high end (Figure 14-14).

Use a standard 48-inch carpenter's level. If the table is level, the bubble will be exactly between the two hash marks on the cylinder of the level. If one end is high, the bubble will be divided by the hash mark on the high end.

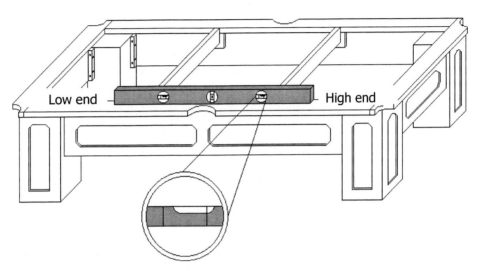

Low end   High end

Figure 14-14 *Determine the high end*

The high end must be leveled side-to-side first. To do that, set the level across the high end of the table (Figure 14-15). For tables with screw-in levelers, screw out (down) the one needed to raise the low leg of the high end of the table. If the table does not have levelers, the low leg must be shimmed. Shims can be any flat non-compressible material like wood, plywood, paneling, asphalt floor tile, or pasteboard, and should vary in thickness between $^1/_{16}$ and $^1/_4$ inches.

Trick of the Trade

Corrugated floor runner (available at most hardware stores) is ideal for leg shims. It's easy to cut to match a leg's footprint, doesn't compress, and is adjustable by placing the grooved faces together.

Each shim should be cut to approximately the size of the table leg's footprint, or slightly smaller, but for appearance, it should not be larger.

Add shim until the low side is level with the high side (Figure 14-15)

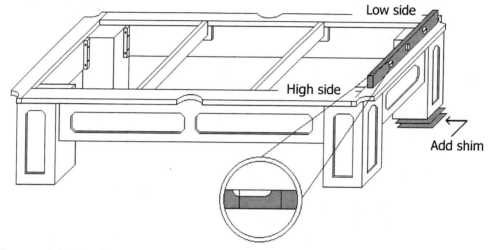

Figure 14-15 *Shim the low leg*

After leveling the high end, level one side of the cabinet or frame from end-to-end using leg levelers or shims, whichever is appropriate (Figure 14-16).

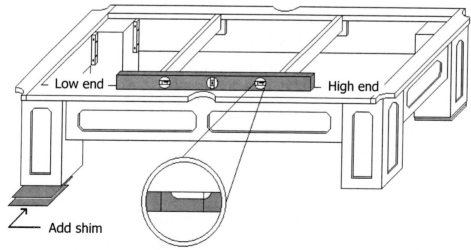

Figure 14-16 *Level end to end*

Trick of the Trade

All four legs should not be shimmed. The leg that began as the HIGH LEG should always remain on the floor or at its lowest position if it is adjustable.

If that leg becomes low during the leveling process, too many shims or too much adjustment has been added to the other legs and should be removed or lowered.

Next, level across the low end of the table (Figure 14-17). When this is done, double-check the entire table. Sometimes leveling one end throws the other end off. Continue until the table is level, or as near level as possible. Often, if the table isn't perfectly flat, it is necessary to split the difference between one side or end and the other, say, within an eighth of an inch or so.

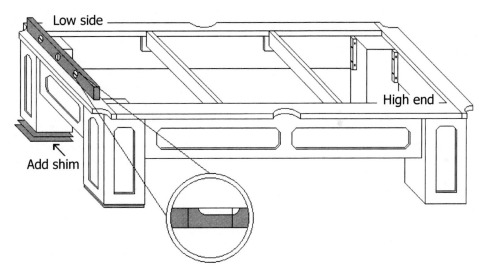

Figure 14-17 *Level across low end*

Words of Experience

Some time ago, I was recovering a table for a young couple in Scottsdale. The husband ran to the store while his wife stayed home to baby-sit their newborn and me. The heat was turned up in the house because of the baby.

The table, old and worn out, needed repairs beyond recovering, but, at this point in their lives, the couple did not have the means to do more.

I had to use extremely long staples to insure a solid grip in the deteriorating tacking strips that were soft and full of holes from countless previous coverings. As I struggled with pulling the cloth around the pulpy wood, stapling close to my thumb, sweat pouring from my face and arms, the young mother suddenly asked if I was hot. I looked up as I pulled the trigger of the electric stapler; it slipped and fired. The staple penetrated the side of my thumb where the nail meets the flesh, and came out at the opposite side of the nail of my index finger. It stapled the cloth between my thumb and finger and the group to the wood.

Tears joined the sweat on my face.

The young lady stared, eyes wide, mouth agape. Then, as I took a pair of pliers and pulled the staple out through the blood, her eyes rolled up and her knees buckled.

At that moment, her husband walked in. I was bleeding on the pool table, his wife lay beside it white as a ghost, and the baby was in her crib wailing.

Pay attention.

SLATE

It is important that the cabinet or frame is level and square, and that all top members be flush with each other before the slate is set on the table.

All slate has a top and bottom, which should not be reversed. There are four ways to determine top from bottom:

1. Each slate will be marked, or have a tacking board affixed to the bottom.

2. The top will likely have shallow circular grooves cut by the surface grinding process; the underside will be smoother looking but it will not necessarily be flat.

3. Each pocket cutout of the topside should have a large and smooth radius curving into the pocket.

4. Slate that is secured to the platform with screws will have countersunk screw holes on the topside.

THREE-PIECE SLATE

To install a three-piece slate set, determine first which slate goes at the head and which at the foot end of the table. Most three-piece slate sets are matched and precision ground as a set, so must be assembled in their matched order. The slate will be marked or numbered on the face or by dimples at the edge of each piece where the seams butt together (see Figure 8-16).

Slate that is not marked is not normally a matched set and, therefore, the end pieces can be interchanged without problems.

Position all three slate pieces on the table. Dowelled and pinned slate might have to be raised at one end or the other to align and set the pins. Measure around the periphery to insure that each slate overhangs the frame equally on both sides and both ends. This also squares the slate to the frame.

Often, beam and slat and board frames have predrilled slate screw holes for machine screws that pass through the frame and are attached with a nut and washer. These frames are mass-produced and the holes do not always align without separating the slate seams. If this is the case, simply redrill the holes using the slate as a template, and a drill bit slightly larger than the screw.

Wood screws, however, secure most slate (Figure 15-1). If the table has been assembled before, slate screw holes will be present in the platform. Using an awl or small Phillips head screwdriver, simply align these holes with the holes in the slate.

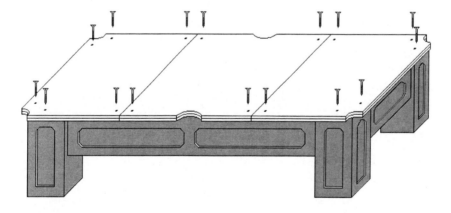

Figure 15-1 *Slate screws*

If the table has never been assembled, pilot holes should be drilled into the platform to insure that the slate screws go in without stripping the heads or splitting the platform. Assuming $^1/_4$-inch diameter slate screws are being used, drill $^1/_8$ to $^3/_{16}$ inch pilot holes (the denser the platform material the larger the pilot hole).

Insert and tighten all slate screws to pull the slates to the platform snugly. This is important and must be done to insure a solid starting point before beginning the leveling process.

Also, some platform boards are so poorly constructed that they will hold a wood screw only long enough to get the cloth on the table. Once the rails are tightened, the screws will pull loose causing the

Trick of the Trade

A small amount of dry bar soap on the wood screw threads will help them turn smoothly and easily.

slate to misalign. This shortcoming can be somewhat corrected in two ways. One, simply replace the wood screws with machine screws, passing them through the tacking board and platform board, and fastening them with fender washers and lock nuts (slate 1 in Figure 15-2).

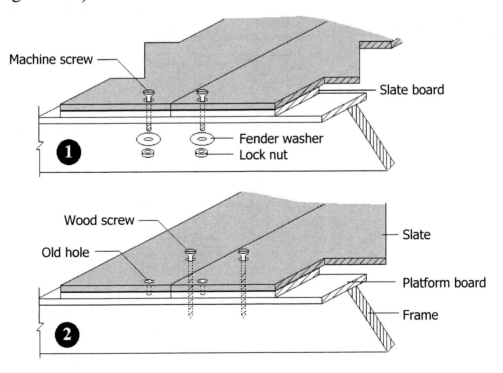

Figure 15-2 *Replace slate screws*

The other correction possibility is to redrill the slate so the slate screws go directly into the table frame (slate 2 in Figure 15-2). This method is probably the better of the two. However, the screws and holes will have to be filled. Slate drilling and screw hole filling instructions are covered later in this Chapter.

Level Slate

After the screws are secure, the top of the slates must be aligned flush, with no runoff in relation to each other. The concern is not that the slate is level at this time, but that each piece is flush with the others and that they are *lying on the same plane*. Once this has been accomplished, the table and slate pieces can be leveled as a unit, if necessary.

The best technique to check for slate misalignment is to hold a straight edge across the seam where two slates meet and look beneath it, between it and the slate. A carpenter's level tilted slightly on edge works fine (Figure 15-3). If a four-foot straight edge or carpenter's level is used, look each seam individually, or, if a six-foot tool is used, look at both seams at the same time.

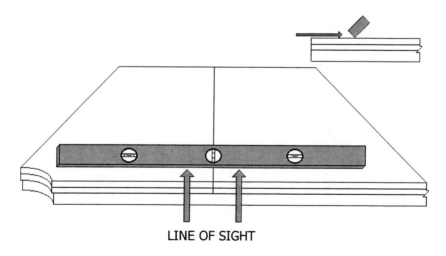

LINE OF SIGHT

Figure 15-3 *Look between the slate and the carpenter's level*

Slate height differences or misalignments can be judged by the gap between the straightedge and the slate. Slate pieces must align to within .005 inches (approximately the thickness of a couple sheets of paper) of each other to meet BCA specifications. Although it is not likely to obtain this kind of accuracy along the entire length of a seam, getting it as close as possible by compromising the adjustments along the seam is possible and advisable. Having two positions off by .006 is better than one at .012. Also, these specifications are given here as references only. Measuring each gap or wave along the seam to determine that it is within tolerances is not necessary. Simply peer between the straight edge and the slate, and adjust the slate until there is no or very little gap between them, and there is no difference between the heights of the two pieces of slate.

A straight edge across a seam will show any one or all of the following four states of alignment or misalignment:

1. The slate pieces will be flush.

2. One slate will be thinner or thicker then the others.

3. Portions of one or both end slate pieces will be low in relation to the center slate.

4. Some portion of the center slate will be low in relation to an end slate.

Each of the four states is discussed fully later. Meanwhile, be aware that around the table all states might exist in varying degrees at the same time. It is also possible that correcting one situation will cause one of the others to occur. Also, the seam on one side of a table could be flush while the other side is not. So it is imperative to check, recheck, and correct at least the six positions adjacent to the slate screws along the side and center of both seams shown in Figure 15-4.

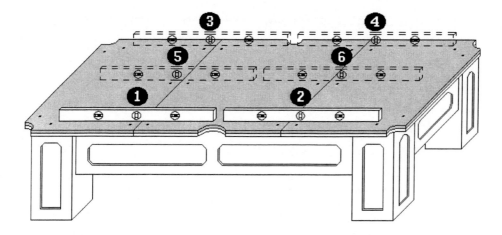

Figure 15-4 *Check at least three positions on each seam*

Because the slate pieces can be severely out of alignment, bowed, or sagging, checking the seams between the slate screws may be wise also. That is, checking in ten places instead of six, with the additional four being between positions 1-5, 3-5, 2-6, and 4-6 in Figure 15-4.

Also, check across the slate, side-to-side, to make sure they are not bowing or sagging that way. If they are, refer to "Warped Slates" later in this chapter.

To correct for slate misalignment, start with the high slate and lift any low slate to the same height. This is why the slate screws must be tightened first—to decide which is truly the high slate. Shims or wedges are used to raise low slates. Shims can be pieces of thin wood, playing cards, sheet metal, or anything that is flat and thin. However, wedges work fine and are much easier to use because of their infinite and minute adjustment possibilities. A few table manufacturers provide slate leveling shims with their tables, but slate wedges can also be purchased from most pool table supply stores. Carpenters' door or framing shims also work fine, and can be purchased from any lumberyard or hardware store. Long, thin, and wide wedges with a gradual taper are superior to short, narrow ones that taper rapidly.

Loosen the slate screws of the low slate and drive a wedge between the slate and the slate platform to force the slate up. Position the wedge approximately one inch from the seam, close to the slate screw. If the tacking board is part of the slate, the wedge must be placed between the tacking board and platform. If, on the other hand, the tacking board is also the platform, or if no tacking board is present, the wedge must be placed directly beneath the slate (Figure 15-5).

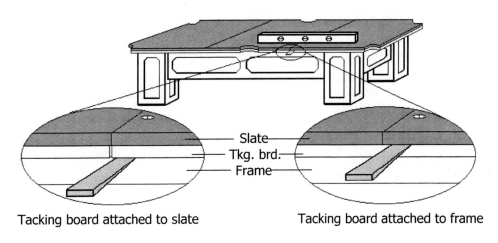

Slate
Tkg. brd.
Frame

Tacking board attached to slate   Tacking board attached to frame

Figure 15-5 *Wedge between the slate and the frame*

If the platform board beneath the slate is thin or weak and bends downward when wedged, drive the wedges outward from beneath the table where the platform, cabinet, or frame is more solid.

Adjustments on dowelled and pinned slate sets must be done slowly and with care. It is possible to break the slate around the dowels by holding one piece down and wedging the other up.

First State

The first of the four states described above is that of *complete alignment*, however unlikely. This occurs when the slate pieces at all six positions along the seams are flush to each other and all three slate pieces are lying on the same plane (Figure 15-6). Figure 15-6 shows positions 1 and 2. Positions 3-4, and 5-6 (Figure 15-4) must also be flush. When this occurs, simply fill the seams and slate screw holes, and go on with the assembly (see "Filling Slate Seams" later in this Chapter).

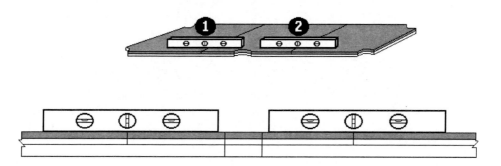

Figure 15-6 *Slates are flush*

Caution

Check one side (both seams at position 1 and 2 in Figure 15-4) of all three slate pieces at the same time. Then check the other side, both seams at position 3 and 4, then the center at positions 5 and 6. It is imperative that the slate pieces are brought flush in some such order. The edges of two seams and all three slate pieces must be flush simultaneously. When the center slate is changed at one seam, it will affect the other seam, so both must be checked and corrected at the same time.

Second State

The second state is one of *misalignment* and occasionally occurs when a slate or tacking board (or portion of the frame) is thinner, or thicker, than the others (Figure 15-7). In this situation, all the screws of the low slate must be loosened, and then wedges must be driven beneath each of its corners until it comes up flush with the others. Figure 15-7 shows positions 1 and 2 only. Positions 3-4, and 5-6 (Figure 15-4) must also be checked and corrected.

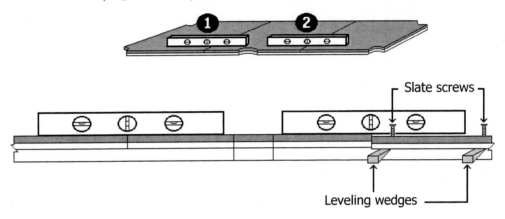

Figure 15-7 *One end slate is low*

Third State

The third state of *misalignment* happens when one or both end slate pieces are lower or pitched low toward the ends of the table (Figure 15-8). This generally occurs because the cabinet or frame is bowed. In this case, loosen the end screws only and drive wedges beneath the slate at the low end, or ends, until the slate pieces are flush with the others. Figure 15-8 shows positions 1 and 2 only. As before, positions 3-4, and 5-6 (as depicted in Figure 15-4) must also be checked and corrected.

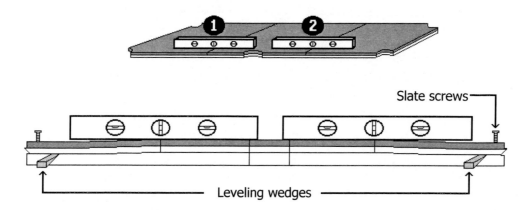

Figure 15-8 *Bowed frame*

Fourth State

The forth state of *misalignment*—and the most likely occurrence—is that the center slate will be lower than the ends (Figure 15-9). This usually happens because the center of the cabinet or frame has sagged. In this instance, the end slates will also pitch low toward the center. Loosen the screws along the seams, and drive wedges beneath the center and end slate pieces, at the seams, until all slate pieces are flush with each other. Figure 15-9 shows positions 1 and 2 only. Also, positions 3-4, and 5-6 (as depicted in Figure 15-4) must also be checked and corrected.

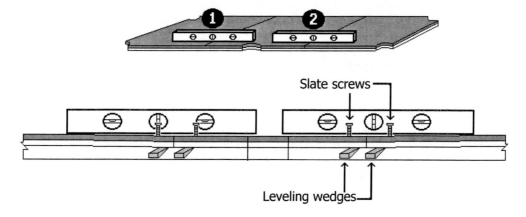

Figure 15-9 *Sagged frame*

In all the above states of *misalignment,* as the slate pieces are being wedged flush, tighten the slate screws until they become secure when the slate pieces are flush. If the screws are tightened after a slate is wedged flush, the slate will probably be pulled low again. So, tighten and wedge at the same time, in small adjustments.

As mentioned above, level the outside edges of both seams, and then check the center. If the outside edges are flush but the center is not, loosen the center slate screw—if there is one—of the low slate pieces. Crawl beneath the table and drive a wedge beneath the low slate, next to the slate screw, until it is flush; then tighten the screw.

If no center screws are present, driving a wedge between the slate and the center frame member at the low point can raise a low or sagging slate. However, if a slate is high or bowed, center screws should be added at the center frame member. Place the screw approximately 1 inch in from the seam's edge to prevent cracking and chipping. For drilling instructions, see "Bowed Slate" later in this Chapter.

Wood can bow, warp, shrink, and compress, so do not be too concerned if only one wedge is needed on one corner of a slate while three or more, or none, are used along the opposite side. Just do what it takes to make the slate pieces flush with each other while they are setting on the same plane.

Also, if two corners of the same edge of a piece of slate have been raised, insert another wedge in the middle, between the two corner wedges, to prevent the slate from sagging.

Once the slate pieces are flush, check the overall table to insure that it is level. Occasionally, especially on carpet, the weight of the slate will cause the table to settle out of level. Re-level the table in the same manner in which the cabinet or frame was leveled initially: find the high end, level it side-to-side, level end-to-end, then level the low end side-to-side.

WARPED SLATE

Slate, a metamorphic rock, cannot only crack and split, but it can also warp.

To check for slate warpage, lay a carpenter's level (or a straight edge) across the middle of the slate, side-to-side, end-to-end, and corner-to-corner. Tilt the level slightly on edge and look beneath it, between it and the slate (see Figure 15-2). If one or more gentle peaks and valleys are detected, the slate is wavy and not much can be done about it short of regrinding. However, one large peak or valley usually shows a slate that has sagged or bowed. Some warpage, if not too severe, can be corrected.

Sagged Slate

Sagging slate can often be corrected simply by driving a wedge between the slate and a stiff frame member at the low position of the sag (Figure 15-10). This is particularly simple on a three-piece slate table on which the slate perimeter is already screwed to the slate platform, and the cabinet or frame members are stout enough to force the slate up when wedged.

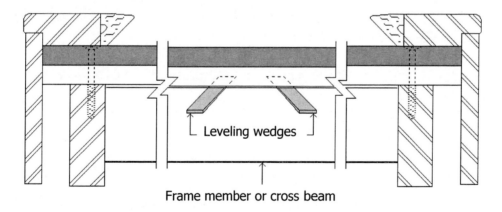

Figure 15-10 *Wedge up sagging slate*

On one-piece slate tables, the slate usually floats or is held in place by the rails only. With these tables, the edges must be secured before the slate can be flexed to a flatter configuration. If perimeter screws are required, follow the drilling instructions in the following "Bowed Slate" section.

Bowed Slate

A bowed slate is one in which the middle is raised higher than the edges. Gravity makes this a rare occurrence, but it can happen. A bowed slate is difficult to correct because it requires drilling at least one screw hole somewhere in the middle of the slate and forcing the slate down with a screw, and this can only be done if the frame or frame member is present and strong enough that it does not pull up instead. So, if the slate must be drilled, pick a spot above a stiff frame member, but as close to the top of the bow as possible.

Trick of the Trade

If necessary, 2 x 4 or 2 x 6 inch frame members can be added. They should be made of hard, dense wood, and must be as long as the slate is wide to properly pull the slate down.

Assuming a $^1/_4$ x 3-inch wood screw will be used, countersink a hole approximately $^1/_4$ inch into the slate, using a $^1/_2$ -inch masonry bit. Then, with a $^5/_{16}$ -inch masonry bit, drill the rest of the way through the slate. If there is a slate tacking board, drill the same size hole through it. Next, drill a $^1/_8$ to $^3/_{16}$ - inch pilot hole into the slate platform or frame member (the denser the wood the larger the pilot hole).

All slate chips must be removed from between the slate and platform or frame member. Either move the slate and sweep beneath it or, if that is not possible, use a length of wire or hacksaw blade to fish the chips out. If the debris is not removed, the slate cannot be pulled down flat.

The $^1/_4$ x 3-inch wood screw should pass easily through the slate and tacking board, then screw firmly into the frame member in order to pull the slate down (Figure 15-11).

The screw head and counter sink can be filled with seam filler to get a smooth playing surface (see the next section, "Filling Slate Seams" below).

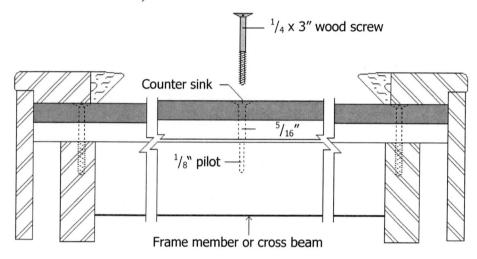

Figure 15-11 *Bowed slate*

FILLING SLATE SEAMS

Imperfections, chips, screw holes, and slate seams can be filled with several materials. The most common three, in order of popularity, are water putty, bees' wax, and auto body filler.

Auto body filler is an excellent and permanent slate seam material. However, it must be mixed, applied, and smoothed quickly because once it dries, expect a considerable amount of sanding and clean up.

Bees' wax is the most forgiving of the three materials in that it remains soft and does not chip, crack, shrink, or become powder. Nevertheless, it is also difficult to apply since it must be melted to a putty consistency, usually with a torch, then applied before it hardens again. No sanding is required if the melted wax is smoothed before it dries.

Water putty is the most widely used material for slate seams simply because it is easy to use. It begins as a powder, which is mixed with water to form putty. Water putty dries in a few minutes, but allows plenty of time for filling and smoothing. If applied properly, no sanding is required, but it can be easily sanded if needed. Once dry, it is almost as hard as the slate itself, but will powder and separate if it gets wet.

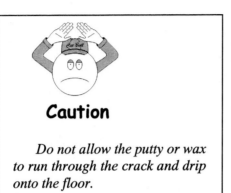

Caution

Do not allow the putty or wax to run through the crack and drip onto the floor.

To use any of the three materials, follow the mixing instruction on their respective containers. Once the material is in a putty state spread it as smooth as possible with a 4-inch putty knife. If the cracks of the seams are wide, force some putty about $^1/_4$ inch into them before wiping the putty smooth (Figure 15-12).

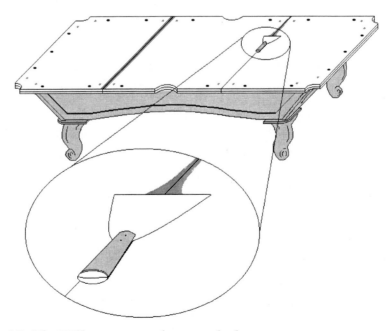

Figure 15-12 *Fill seams and screw holes.*

Fill all holes, chips, and cracks that will be in the playing area. Those that will lie beneath the rails (less than four inches from the edge) after they are installed do not have to be filled.

Trick of the Trade

If water putty filler is used to fill screw holes, pack the holes with dry putty powder first, then spread putty on top of the powder. Once dry, the hardened putty will stay in place, but if it has to be removed later, it will dislodge as a plug with little chipping or drilling required.

If the slate pieces are not flush and the seam material is "feathered" to fill the difference in height, a slight ball jump will be created. Therefore, if the seam material is spreading in a feathered manner, before it dries, gently drive a wedge beneath the low slate to bring it up to the height of the high slate. Then wipe the seam again with the putty knife so only the crack is filled with seam material. With today's slate, however, eliminating all feathering is not always possible, but keeping it paper-thin is. BCA regulations allow .005 inches of misalignment.

After the putty dries, use a sandpaper block to smooth out any large humps, bumps, or tool marks, if necessary. This process does not have to be perfect, small imperfections will not be noticed once the cloth is stretched across the slate. Brush all loose debris from the slate, but washing it is not required.

ONE-PIECE SLATE

To install a one-piece slate, simply set it on, or in, the cabinet or frame and attach by whatever means provided. Most one-piece slates are held in place by only the rails. Also, most one-piece slates are covered with billiard cloth before they are installed (see Chapter 17).

Once the slate is in place, the table should be level, assuming the cabinet or frame has been pre-leveled. Because of the weight of the slate, however, the table could settle uneven. If so, re-leveling the table is done in the same manner as shown in Chapter 13, and the following section, "Fine-Tune the Levelness."

It is conceivable that a one-piece slate could be sagged or bowed depending on the slate thickness, density, and the quality of the table (see "Warped Slate" above).

FINE-TUNE
THE LEVELNESS

Using a pool cue, gently cue a ball across (side-to-side) the bare slate; do not use english (see *A Rookie's Guide to Playing Winning Pool* on how english affects the ball). Using a cue is important, instead of hand rolling the ball, to prevent unwanted ball spin. Watch to see if the ball rolls toward the head or foot before it falls from the table. The ball will, of course, roll toward the low end. Shim beneath the legs, or adjust the levelers, of that end until the ball rolls true. Careful, though, it should not take much adjustment.

Next, slowly cue a ball from one end to the other along both sides of the table. If a low corner is detected, raise that corner by shimming beneath that leg, or by adjusting the leg leveler. Then cue a ball toward the other end to insure that the ball rolls true in that direction.

If the ball rolls true on bare slate, then, after the cloth has been installed, no roll-off should be detected other than a small amount of cloth (nap) roll as the ball slows to a stop. BCA regulations allow for one ball diameter roll-off for the length of the table. Any table can easily be leveled to beat that tolerance.

Furthermore, this process of leveling with a ball can be repeated with the cloth on the table as often as needed. At some point, though, lowering a high corner is advisable instead of raising a low corner.

A table should never be lifted from any part except the cabinet or frame. Rails, aprons, pockets, and slate screws are not designed to support the weight of the entire table. Several table jacks are available, but any short automobile jack will work. Jack only at the center of a side or end of the cabinet or frame (Figure 15-13).

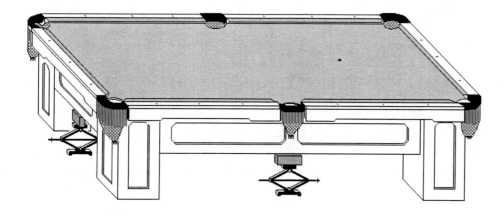

Figure 15-13 *Table jacking points*

CLOTH CUTTING GUIDE

Undoubtedly the most difficult segment of pool table installation is replacing the cloth. However, that does not mean that it cannot be done by anyone who sets his or her mind to it, especially if the instructions in this Chapter and Chapters 16 and 17 are followed.

To begin, because of the manufacturing process, most billiard cloth is considered to have a face (upside) and a back (downside), and must be installed face up. Some cloth will work upside down, but the backside tends to pill more than the front. To be on the safe side, simply install it right side up.

Except for cloth that is backed with vinyl, telling the difference is extremely hard, if not impossible. Some mills are clever enough to mark the back, but most are not. Generally, though, the face will have a slight sheen, but even that's often hard to detect.

Trick of the Trade

When the cloth is in a roll or bolt, the face will be up when unrolled. If folded, the face will be the two halves that are touching at the last unfolding.

CLOTH MEASUREMENTS

Occasionally billiard cloth can be purchased as a kit with the rail cloth pieces already separated from the bed cloth, and with the upside or downside marked. Usually, though, the material comes in one large piece, leaving the installer or mechanic with the responsibility of cutting the rail cloth pieces from the bed cloth, and remembering which is up and which is down.

Some rail cloth pieces are cut from the side of the bed cloth and some from the end, depending on the cloth and size of the pool table. The word "cut" is used loosely here because non-directional billiard cloth can be torn straight, end-to-end and side-to-side, and it is by far the most widely used cloth. Simply mark the edge where it is to be torn, cut the first couple of inches, and rip it the rest of the way. Directional, worsted, and backed cloth, on the other hand, may not rip straight; use scissors and care.

Caution

When using vinyl-backed cloth for rails, the backing must be removed from the rail cloth and only the rail cloth. Separating the rail cloth pieces from the bed cloth first is therefore necessary.

Trick of the Trade

Before cutting standard, non-backed cloth, use a felt-tipped marker to mark the back of the cloth. Also, as the rail cloth is being cut, fold each piece so the face is folded in. This prevents soiling the face or installing the cloth upside down.

The yardage of cloth required varies with the size of the pool table. Yardage is usually figured only as close as the nearest $^1/_4$ or $^1/_3$ yard, and not necessarily to the inch.

Table 16-1 shows the yardage needed for the bed and rails of most common size pool tables, using standard 62- or 63-inch wide cloth.

TABLE SIZE (in feet)	SLATE SIZE (in inches)	DIRECTIONAL (in linear yards)	NON-DIRECTIONAL (in linear yards)
Rebound table	32 x 48	1.50	1.50
3 x 6	$5^1/_2$ x $67^1/_2$	2.25	2.25
3 x 6 OS	39 x 75	2.25	2.25
$3^1/_2$ x 7 (1psc)	$40^1/_4$ x $77^1/_2$	2.33	2.33
$3^1/_2$ x 7 (1psc)	42 x 82	2.33	2.33
$3^1/_2$ x 7 (1psc)	43 x 83	2.33	2.33
$3^1/_2$ x 7 OS	46 x 85	3.50	2.75
44" x 88" (1psc)	$47^1/_2$ x $91^1/_2$	4.00	3.00
44" x 88" (3psc)	51 x 95	4.00	3.00
4 x 8	50 x 96	4.00	3.00
4 x 8 OS	53 x 99	4.25	3.50
$4^1/_2$ x 9	54 x 104	4.33	3.66
$4^1/_2$ x 9 OS	57 x 107	4.50	4.25
5 x 10	60 x 116	5.00	4.33
5 x 10 OS	63 x 119	5.50	4.50

Table 16-1 *Cloth yardage needed for bed and rails*

NON-DIRECTIONAL CLOTH

Figures 16-1 through 16-7 show how to cut the rail cloth pieces from standard width non-directional cloth for most common size pool tables. Ideally, rail cloth pieces should be 6 inches wide and at least 4 inches longer than the length of the rails. Pieces $5^1/_2$ inches wide can be used without problems and should be considered for 62-inch wide and narrower cloth.

$3^1/_2$ X 7 Standard Tables
Cut all six rail cloth pieces from the side of the material.

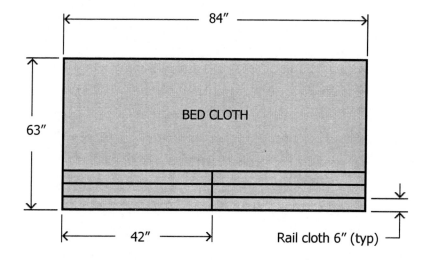

Figure 16-1 *2.33 yards*

$3^{1}/_{2}$ X 7 Oversize Tables

Cut four rail cloth pieces from the side and two from the end.

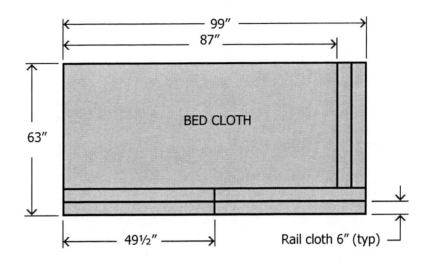

Figure 16-2 *2.75 yards*

4 X 8 Standard and 44 X 88 Tables

Cut four rail cloth pieces from the side and two from the end.

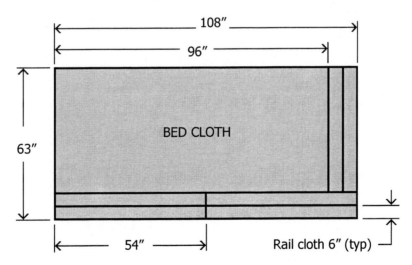

Figure 16-3 *3 yards*

4 X 8 Oversize Tables

Cut two rail cloth pieces from the side and four from the end.

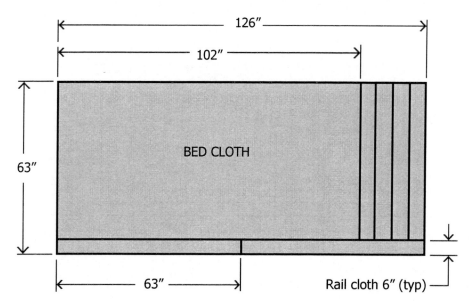

Figure 16-4 *3.5 yards*

4¹/₂ X 9 Standard Tables

Cut two rail cloth pieces from the side and four from the end.

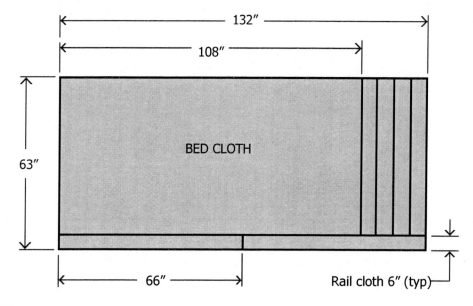

Figure 16-5 *3.66.yards*

$4^1/_2$ X 9 Oversize Tables

Cut all six rail cloth pieces from the end of the material.

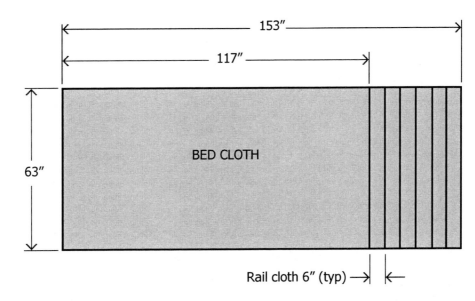

Figure 16-6 *4.25 yards*

5 X 10 Standard Tables

Cut all six rail cloth pieces from the end of the material.

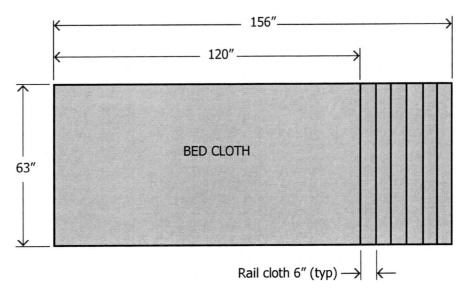

Figure 16-7 *4.33 yards*

5 X 10 Oversize Tables

Cut all six rail cloth pieces from the end of the material.

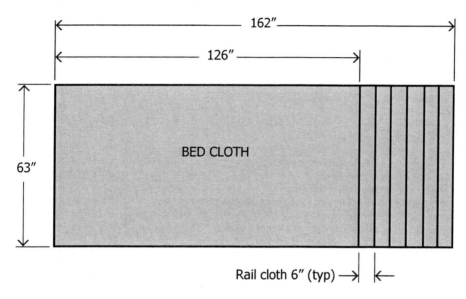

Figure 16-8 *4.5 yards*

6 X 12 and Larger Tables

Standard width billiard cloth will not stretch from side-to-side on 12-foot and larger tables. Cloth for these tables has to be special ordered. However, 6-inch rail cloth will still work, and all six pieces can be cut from the end of the material. To figure the yardage needed, measure the length and width of the slate, then add another yard for the six rail cloth pieces.

The exception is carom tables of any size because the two side rails are as long as the table bed (See Figure 16-16). If the rail cloth pieces cannot be cut from the side of the material, they must be ordered separately. The two end-rail cloth pieces can be cut from the end of the material.

DIRECTIONAL CLOTH

Because the nap of directional cloth is to lie from the head of the pool table toward the foot, rail cloth pieces cannot be cut from across the end of the cloth. Billiard table cloth suppliers should be equipped to sell only the amount of cloth needed for the job (bed cloth plus six rail cloth pieces). If not, some of the rail cloth pieces must be taken from an excess cut of fabric.

To figure the amount of directional cloth required from standard width cloth, simply measure the length of the slate and add 3 inches for gluing or stapling. Then, because of nap direction, some rail cloth pieces must be cut from some source other than the bed cloth. This other material must be equal to the length of the rails plus 4 to 6 inches. Add the two measurements to get the total yardage.

Figures 16-8 through 16-12 show how to cut standard width directional cloth for most common size tables.

Caution

Directional and worsted cloth will not rip straight, use scissors.

$3^1/_2$ X 7 Standard and Smaller Tables

Cut all six rail cloth pieces from the side of the material.

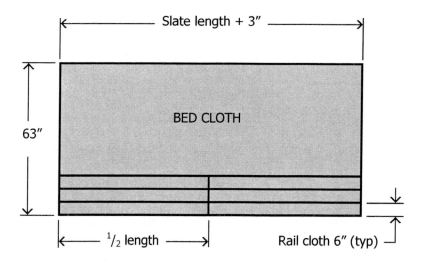

Figure 16-9 *2.33 yards or less*

$3^1/_2$ X 7 Oversize Tables

Cut four rail cloth pieces from the side and two from the excess piece.

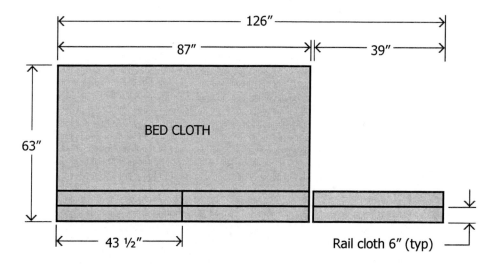

Figure 16-10 *3.5 yards*

4 X 8 Standard and 44 X 88 Tables

Cut four rail cloth pieces from the side and two from the excess piece.

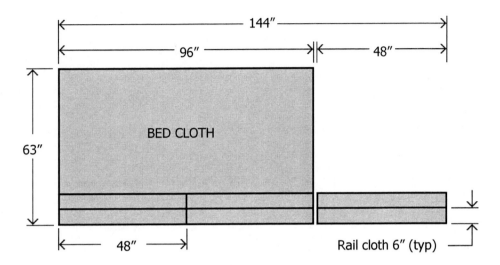

Figure 16-11 *4 yards*

4 X 8 Oversize Tables

Cut two rail cloth pieces from the side and four from the excess piece.

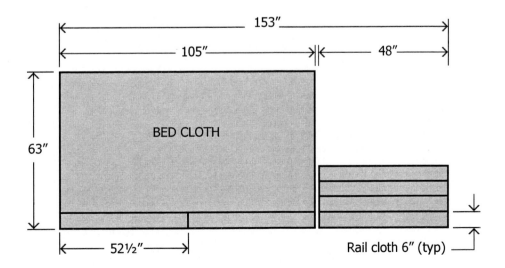

Figure 16-12 *4.25 yards*

4$^1/_2$ X 9 Standard Tables

Cut two rail cloth pieces from the side and four from the excess piece.

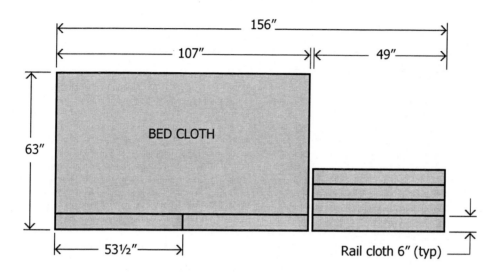

Figure 16-13 *4.33 yards*

4$^1/_4$ X 9 Oversize Tables

Cut all six rail cloth pieces from the excess piece of the material.

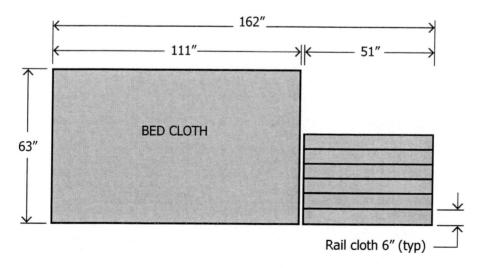

Figure 16-14 *4.5 yards*

5 X 10 Standard and Oversize Tables

Cut all six rail cloth pieces from the excess piece of material.

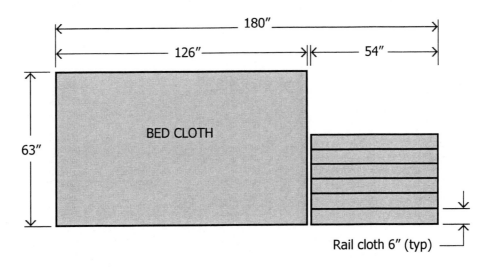

Figure 16-15 *5 yards*

6 X 12 and Larger Tables

Standard width billiard cloth will not stretch from side-to-side on 12-foot and larger tables. Cloth for these tables must be special ordered. Six-inch rail cloth will still work, but because of nap direction, all six pieces must be cut *with* the nap, which usually means from their own source. Measure the length and width of the slate to figure how much bed cloth material is needed. Measure the length of the rails and add 4 to 6 inches to obtain the rail cloth needed. Add the two measurements to get the total yardage.

Carom tables pose a slightly different problem. The two side rails are as long as the table bed (Figure 16-16), so three 6-inch strips must be cut from the side of the material, for length and to maintain nap direction, and one of the strips cut in half, giving you two side and two end pieces. If the bed cloth isn't wide enough, then all four rail cloth pieces must be ordered separately.

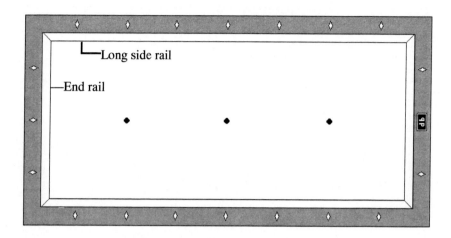

Figure 16-16 *Carom table*

WIDE CLOTH

The rails from wider cloth, like 78-inch worsted, can all be cut from the side of the cloth. Cut all six rail cloth pieces from the side of the material. **For carom tables, leave two of the strips full length.**

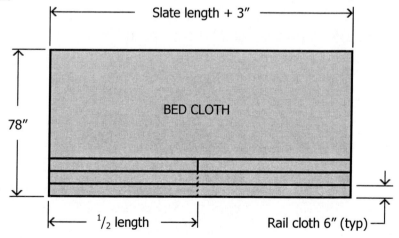

Figure 16-17 Wide cloth

BED CLOTH

Because of the variety of pool table styles, types, and manufacturers, including the cloth installation of each specific table would be almost impossible. However, all cloth replacements can be categorized into four general groups: regulation tables with slate backing boards, regulation tables without slate backing boards, coin-operated tables, and one catchall group for non-regulation tables This includes pool, snooker, and carom tables.

(1) Regulation tables **with backed slate** are all three-piece slate tables on which the rails attach directly to the slate, and the cloth is stapled to the tacking (backing) board.

(2) Regulation tables **without backed slate** are all three-piece slate tables on which the rails attach directly to the slate, and the cloth is glued directly to the edge of the slate.

(3) Coin-operated and other one-piece, undersize slate tables.

(4) Non-regulation tables include all non-slate or nonstandard tables.

Bed cloth installation is not particularly complicated, but can be easily "messed up" if two factors are not remembered. One, pull the cloth as tight as feasible to insure a smooth, wrinkle free installation, and two, the cloth should be stretched the same in all directions so the grain or weave is running as straight and square with the table bed as possible.

161

Cloth installation on new and tables being re-covered is virtually the same procedure. For re-covering, after removing the old bed cloth, brush all dust and debris from the slate. Washing the slate is not necessary, but any ridges of dirt or chalk dust should be scraped relatively smooth. Make sure the slates are flush and level, and seams, screw holes, chips, etc. are filled.

REGULATION (BACKED) TABLES

Cutout Padding

To begin, cut six strips of billiard cloth, each at a width that equals the thickness of the slate and slate tacking board, and long enough to wrap each pocket cutout. These can be taken from scrap rail material or the side of the bed cloth. Using contact cement or spray adhesive, glue one strip into each of the six pocket cutouts, about $1/4$ inch below the top edge of the slate (Figure 17-1). This will leave a $1/4$-inch overhang at the bottom of the cutout. Slit the overhang in three or four places so it will wrap the tacking board for a smooth edge.

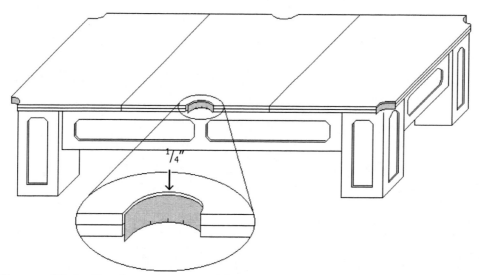

Figure 17-1 *Pocket cutout padding*

Attach Bed Cloth Ends

Next, lay the bed cloth *face up* on the table, leaving an equal amount hanging over each side and end.

The nap of directional cloth is usually laid toward the foot of the table. Except for professional tournament play, this is not particularly critical, but balls roll faster "with the nap," and experienced players allow for it. The

Caution

Pliers make stretching easier, but can also rip the cloth. Use them with discretion.

direction of the nap can be detected by lightly stroking the cloth toward one end. If the nap lies smooth, that is the direction that goes toward the foot of the table. If the nap ruffles, that is the direction that goes toward the head.

Non-directional cloth can lie in either direction.

Starting at the head of the table, staple the middle of the bed cloth to the tacking board, then stretch the cloth toward each side of that end of the table and staple there, staying about 2 inches from the pocket cutouts (Figure 17-2).

Trick of the Trade

By not stapling the cloth within 2 inches of the pocket cutouts allows it to later pull smoothly and easily around and into the cutouts.

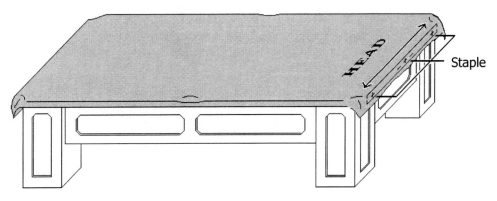

Figure 17-2 *Attach one end first*

For right now, staple the cloth in only those three places: middle and both sides. Use three or four staples in each area, and crossing a couple staples will give them added strength.

At the foot of the table, using hands or pliers, stretch the middle of the cloth tight (Figure 17-3). Do not let up while attaching. Cloth will begin to loosen almost immediately and over time can become very loose, so keep it pulled tight.

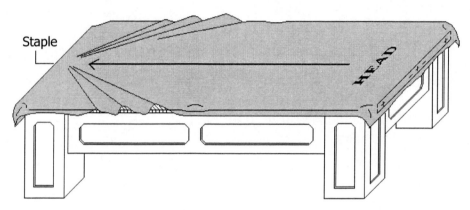

Figure 17-3 *Stretch center to opposite end and attach*

Next, stretch the cloth toward the sides of that end while pulling from the opposite end and parallel with the side of the table. Stretch the cloth tight and staple the sides of that end staying a couple of inches from the pocket cutouts (Figure 17-4). And, again, crossing the staples for added strength.

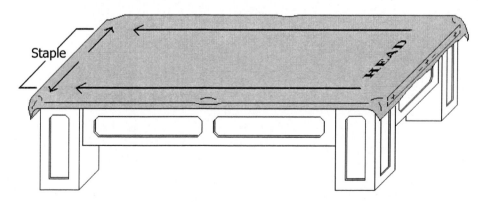

Figure 17-4 *Attach the sides of that end*

Attach Center Pocket Cutouts

At either side of the table, stretch the bed cloth into the center pocket cutout and staple at the bottom edge of, or just beneath, the tacking board (cutout 1 in Figure 17-5). Putting the first staple beneath the tacking board is preferred so the staple doesn't show, although it isn't always possible. Either way, small puckers will occur at the top of the bed, but they will pull out later.

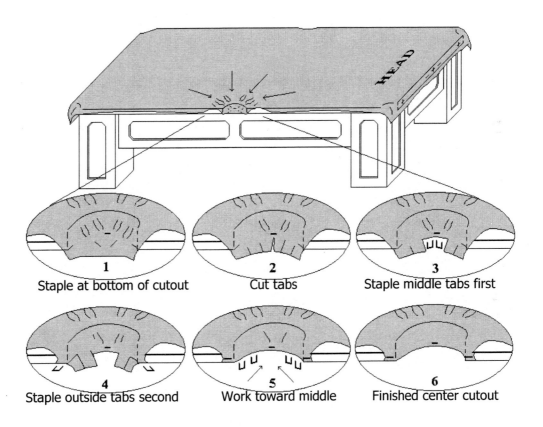

1 Staple at bottom of cutout   2 Cut tabs   3 Staple middle tabs first

4 Staple outside tabs second   5 Work toward middle   6 Finished center cutout

Figure 17-5 *Attach first center pocket cutout*

Slit the cloth down from the staple, below the tacking board (cutout 2 in Figure 17-5), and at two or three other locations, making four to six tabs, each about $^1/_2$ inch wide.

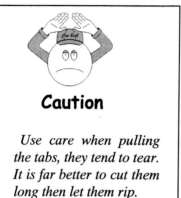

Caution

Use care when pulling the tabs, they tend to tear. It is far better to cut them long then let them rip.

The slits should start at the bottom edge of the slate tacking board so that neither the slate nor the tacking board will show. If this proves to be impossible, let the slits extend upward into the cutout, but not by more than $\frac{1}{2}$ inch. When the slits extend into the cutouts, the padding strips glued there earlier will hide the slate and tacking board, producing a fairly neat pocket cutout. Pull the cloth smooth around the face of the cutout. **Staple the middle two tabs first (cutout 3 in Figure 17-5), then pulling the outside tabs to the edge of the slate will help eliminate some of the bubbles that are on top of the cutout (cutout 4 in Figure 17-5). Next, working from the outside toward the middle will eliminate the puckers in the cutout face (cutout 5 in Figure 17-5).** In some cases it may be necessary to work from the middle toward the outside, just do whichever works better. Again, don't worry about small puckers on top, they will be pulled out later (cut out 6 in Figure 17-5).

At the other side of the table, repeat the process for the second center pocket cutout (Figure 17-6)

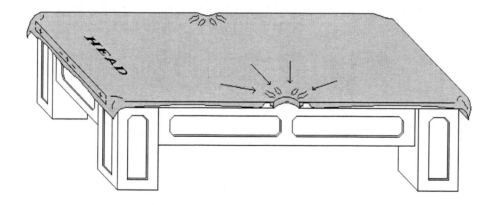

Figure 17-6 Attach second center pocket cutout

Attach Corner Pocket Cutout

For the corner pocket cutouts, start at any of the four corners and draw the cloth along that side, toward the corner pocket cutout, and staple an inch or two from that cutout. The cloth will pull slightly from across the table, but most of it will come from the center pocket and should be pulled tight enough to eliminate most of the puckers on top of the bed, at the center pocket of that side (Figure 17-7). The remainder of the puckers should pull out when the side and ends of the cloth is stretched.

Attach the cloth with three or four staples, crossing them for strength, if necessary. Repeat the process for the remaining three corner cutouts.

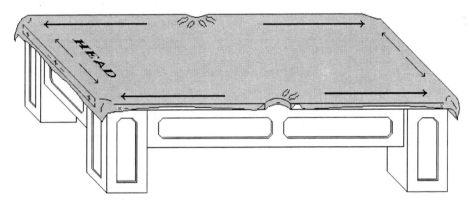

Figure 17-7 *Attach sides at the corners*

To finish the corner pocket cutouts, stretch the cloth into the cutout and staple at the bottom or beneath the tacking board (cutout 1 in Figure 17-8). **You may get a small pucker or "bubble" at the top of the cutout. This bubble should pull out when the outside tabs are stapled.**

Slit the cloth down from the staple, below the tacking board, and at two or three other locations around the cutout to make four to six tabs (cutout 2 in Figure 17-8). The slits should start at the bottom edge of the slate tacking board so that neither the slate nor the tacking board will show. If this proves to be impossible, try not to let the slits extend more than $^1/_2$ inch onto the cutout.

When the slits extend into the cutouts, the padding strips glued there earlier will hide the slate and tacking board, producing an acceptable pocket cutout.

Pull the cloth smooth around the face of the cutout and staple the tabs below the cutout. **Staple the middle two tabs first (cutout 3 in Figure 17-8), then pulling the outside tabs to the edge of the slate should eliminate any bubbles that are on top of the cutout (cutout 4 in Figure 17-8). Next, working from the outside toward the middle will eliminate the puckers in the cutout face (cutout 5 in Figure 17-8).** In some cases it may be necessary to work from the middle toward the outside, just do whichever works better for you and your table.

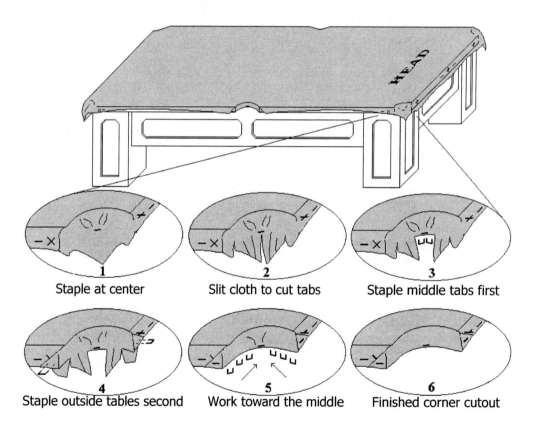

1	2	3
Staple at center	Slit cloth to cut tabs	Staple middle tabs first
4	5	6
Staple outside tables second	Work toward the middle	Finished corner cutout

Figure 17-8 *Attach corner pocket cutouts*

Attach Sides and Ends

Next, stretch the cloth and staple along one side and then the other, stapling every three to four inches. When you do the second side, pull the cloth as tight as possible. Now, stretch and staple the ends (Figure 17-9). This should eliminate the remaining puckers and bubbles at the pocket cutouts. If it doesn't, remove the staples in the pocket cutouts, below the puckers, and relieve the pressure there, then re-staple.

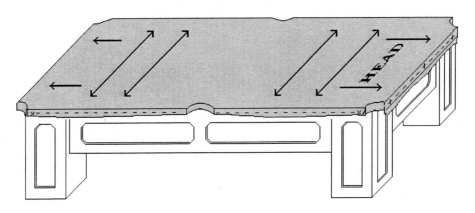

Figure 17-9 *Finish attaching sides and ends*

Caution

Attaching billiard fabric with little or no nap (or a predominate weave) in this manner curves or distorts the cloth's natural weave into the pocket, instead of allowing it to run parallel with the table. This may allow a slow moving ball to follow the weave into the pocket. But for most billiard fabric, it makes little difference.

Trim and Cut Bolt Holes

Trim the excess cloth along the bottom edge of the slate board, below the staples, and reinforce any staple that appears not to be holding by driving another beside it.

Trick of the Trade

Locate the holes from beneath the slate. This guarantees cutting only rail bolt holes.

Finally, cut rail bolt holes in the bed cloth. T-rail tables have bolt holes in the edge of the slate. Flat rail tables have rail bolt holes penetrating the top of the slate (Figure 17-10). Without cutting these holes in the cloth, it is difficult if not impossible to later find the rail lugs when attaching the rails.

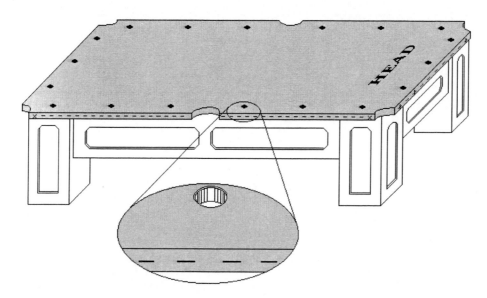

Figure 17-10 *Cut rail bolt holes and trim edges*

REGULATION (UNBACKED) TABLES

Some tables with unbacked slate have slate platforms that extend to the edge of the slate and doubles as slate backing boards. That is, the bed cloth is stapled to the platform. Cover these tables as if they were *backed* slate tables, as shown above.

Other unbacked slate tables have a narrow, more rigid slate platform that does not extend to the edge of the slate (Figure 17-11).

The only purpose of these platforms is to solidly hold the slate in place, and therefore, the cloth is *glued* directly onto the edge of the slate.

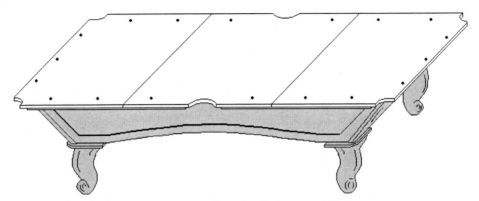

Figure 17-11 *Three-piece unbacked slate tables*

Glue and Attach One End

Lay the bed cloth face up on the table, leaving an equal amount hanging over each side and end, and fold 8 to 10 inches of one end of the cloth up so the underside shows (Figure 17-12).

If possible, cover the cabinet with paper, cardboard, or a drop cloth to prevent glue over spray from settling on it. And newspaper, cardboard, or some similar material spread on top of the bed cloth will also protect it from over spray. Use spray adhesive like 3M brand 77 or 76, or brushable contact cement. All three adhere fine but spray adhesive is the easiest to work with, and 3M 76 withstands high temperatures like summertime garages and so forth.

Spray (or brush) a 2-inch band of glue the full width of the edge of that end of the slate along the top and bottom (Figure 17-12).

Trick of the Trade

Light over spray can usually be peeled off with the sticky side of masking or strapping tape. Persistent over spray can be removed with mineral spirits.

Also, apply a band of glue approximately 4 inches wide along the width of the underside of the bed cloth. Allow all surfaces to become tacky according to specific glue manufactures instructions, usually two to five minutes.

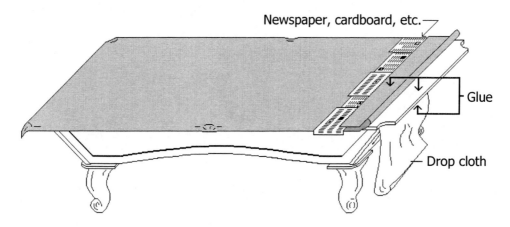

Figure 17-12 *Apply glue to slate and cloth*

Unfold the cloth and attach the *middle of that end* to the top and edge of the slate, letting the end of the cloth overhang, but do not attach the bottom at this time. Stretch the cloth toward each side of that end of the slate and attach, keeping the cloth edge parallel with the edge of the slate (Figure 17-13).

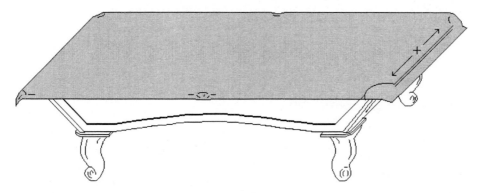

Figure 17-13 *Attach middle then stretch to sides*

From the bottom of the slate, at the pocket cutouts, cut the overhanging cloth at a 45-degree angle down and in. This prevents any excess from wrapping into the pocket cutout.

After cutting the angle, fold the overhanging cloth under the slate and attach it to the bottom, but do not allow the cloth to pucker or crease beneath the slate; it should be smooth to insure a good grip (Figure 17-14).

Caution

Some manufacturers and mechanics glue only the top and edge, while others glue only the bottom and edge. However, it will not harm the table to glue all three surfaces—2" of the top, edge, and 2" of the bottom—to insure that the cloth holds.

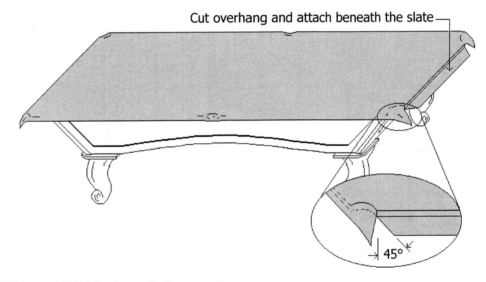

Cut overhang and attach beneath the slate

45°

Figure 17-14 *Attach first end*

Glue and Attach Second End

Protect the other end of the table with a drop cloth, or some such material, and then apply glue to it in the same manner as the first end—edges of slate, approximately 2 inches on top and bottom, and approximately 4 inches along the width of the underside of the cloth (refer back to Figure 17-12).

After the glue has become tacky, stretch the middle tight to that end and attach the top and edge (Figure 17-15). Keep the cloth taut while attaching. Cloth will begin to loosen almost immediately, and over time can become very loose, so it needs to be tight and smooth now.

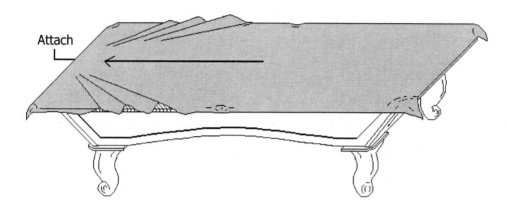

Figure 17-15 *Stretch center and attach*

Next, stretch the cloth toward the sides of that end, pulling parallel with the side of the slate and from the opposite end of the table, and attach to the top and edge of the slate. Again, stretch the cloth tight and smooth while attaching to the top and edge of the slate (Figure 17-16).

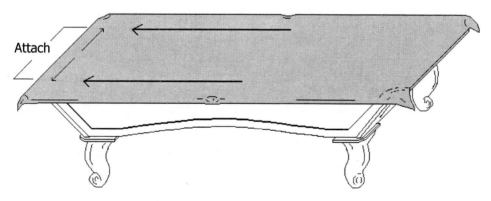

Figure 17-16 *Stretch parallel with slate and attach*

As before, cut the overhanging cloth at a 45-degree angle from the pocket cutouts before attaching beneath the slate (refer back to Figure 17-14), and as before, do not let the cloth pucker or crease beneath the slate.

Glue and Attach One Side

Protect one side of the table with a drop cloth material. Fold 8 to 10 inches of cloth of that side up to expose the underside. Use newspaper, cardboard, drop cloth etc. to protect the top of the cloth from spray. Apply glue to the slate and the underside of the cloth as before. This time include the pocket cutouts in the gluing process (Figure 17-17).

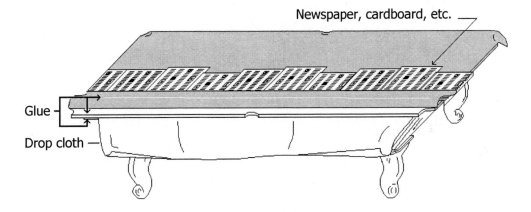

Figure 17-17 *Apply glue to the slate and the cloth*

Unfold the cloth and stretch it along that side of the slate, from the center cutout toward each corner cutout, and attach the ends, next to the corner pocket cutouts—top and edge only (Figure 17-18). Allow the cloth to pucker slightly in the corner pocket cutouts. Attach the remainder of that side, keeping the edge of the cloth parallel with the slate.

Cut the overhang at a 45-degree angle from the pocket cutouts then attach to the bottom of the slate (Figure 17-18).

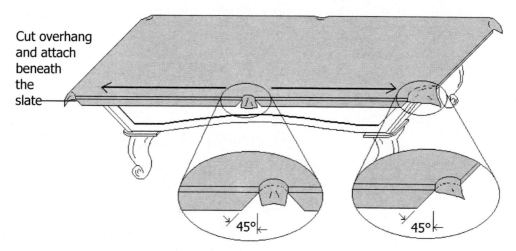

Cut overhang and attach beneath the slate

45°   45°

Figure 17-18 *Attach first side and cut overhang angle*

Glue and Attach Second Side

Glue the other side (refer back to Figure 17-17 and do not forget the drop cloth, etc.). Stretch the bed cloth along that side, first one end, and then the other. This time, however, pull the cloth from across the slate at the same time. Stretch it as tight as possible, try to get a slight pucker in the corner pocket cutouts, and attach only to the top and edges of the slate (Figure 17-19).

Cut the overhang at a 45-degree angle from the pocket cutouts and attach to the bottom of the slate (see Figure 17-18).

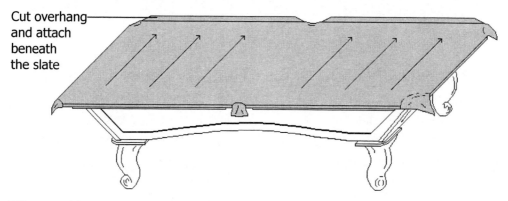

Cut overhang and attach beneath the slate

Figure 17-19 *Attach the other side*

Glue and Attach Pocket Cutouts

To finish, slit the cloth in the pocket cutouts to make four to six tabs depending on the curvature of the cutout—the smaller the radius the more tabs. Try to prevent the slits from extending up past the bottom of the slate. If they do, keep them to within a quarter to a half the thickness of the slate.

Pull each tab tight and attach to the slate edge and bottom (Figure 17-20).

The use of pocket cutout padding (see Figure 17-1) up to half the thickness of the slate may be used behind the tabs to hide the slate and, if used, should be installed

Trick of the Trade

Strapping tape on the bottom surface of the slate, across all of the tabs, will help prevent them from slipping.

before the tabs are attached; however, the gluing surface used for the padding could be crucial in holding the tabs in place.

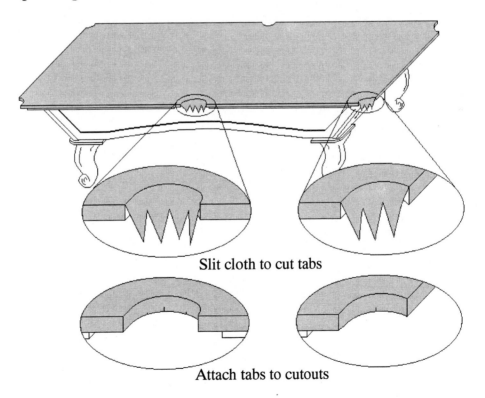

Slit cloth to cut tabs

Attach tabs to cutouts

Figure 17-20 *Cut pocket cutout tabs.*

Trick of the Trade

Locate the holes from beneath the slate. This guarantees cutting only rail bolt holes.

Cut Bolt Holes

Finally, cut rail bolt holes in the bed cloth. Flat rail tables have rail bolt holes penetrating the top of the slate (Figure 17-21). Without cutting these holes in the cloth, it is difficult if not impossible to later find the rail lugs when attaching the rails.

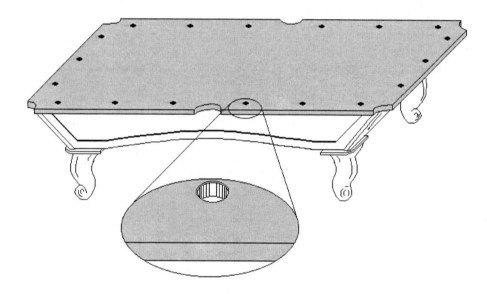

Figure 17-21 *Cut rail bolt holes*

COIN-OPERATED TABLES

The cloth of some coin-operated, one-piece slate tables is stapled to the slate platform. In that case, follow the procedures starting on page 162, as if it were a regulation *backed* slate table. The cloth of some coin-operated, three-piece slate tables is glued to the slate. In that case, follow the procedures starting on page 170, for regulation **unbacked** slate tables. The cloth of most coin-operated, one-piece slate tables is also glued directly to the slate, and following directions should be used for those.

Trick of the Trade

Instead of blocks, 2- or 3-inch PVC pipe also works. This allows the slate to roll along the table for ease of working and cleaning. Use caution, though, and don't let the slate roll off the table.

Usually the slate of most coin-operated tables is removed or simply lifted from the cabinet (see Chapter 7 for dismantling). The slate can be transferred to sawhorses or a workbench, or it can simply be raised and set on 4 x 4 inch blocks or doubled 2 x 4's. Blocks that are 6 to 8 inches shorter than the width of the slate are set on the cross members of the frame below the slate. If 2 x 4's are used, nail them together, with the bottom board longer than the width of the frame and the top board 6 to 8 inches shorter than the width of the slate (Figure 17-22). The idea is to provide ample working space below the slate.

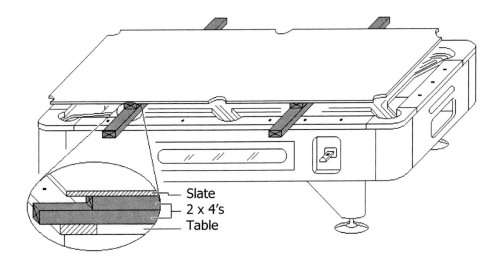

Figure 17-22 *One-piece slate on blocks*

Removing the old cloth from tables that are being re-covered is an easy matter of peeling it off the slate. Brush the bare slate to get rid of dirt and debris. Any ridges of dirt, chalk dust, or glue residue should be scraped relatively smooth, but washing, chemicals, paint thinners, and so forth are not necessary.

When the slate is ready, lay the bed cloth face up on it, leaving an equal amount hanging over each side and end.

The nap of directional cloth should lie toward the foot of the table. Except for professional tournament play, this is not particularly critical; the balls simply roll faster "with the nap." The direction of the nap can be detected by lightly stroking the cloth toward one end. If the nap lies smooth, that is the direction that goes toward the foot of the pool table. If the nap ruffles, that is the direction that goes toward the head.

Non-directional cloth can lie in either direction.

Cover the cabinet, including the internal mechanism of coin-operated tables, with a drop cloth or old billiard cloth to prevent glue over spray from settling on it. Newspaper, cardboard, or some similar material spread on top of the bed cloth will also protect it from over spray.

Fold 8 to 10 inches of one end of the cloth over so that the underside shows (Figure 12-23).

Trick of the Trade

Light over spray can usually be peeled off with the sticky side of masking or strapping tape. Persistent over spray can be removed with mineral spirits.

Glue and Attach One End

Use spray adhesive like 3M brand 76, or brushable contact cement. Both adhere fine but spray adhesive is the easiest to work with. Spray (or brush) a 2-inch band of glue the full width of the edge of one end of the slate along the top and bottom.

Also, apply a band of glue approximately 4 inches wide along the width of the 8 to 10 inches of the underside of the bed cloth that's folded over (Figure 17-23). Allow all surfaces to become tacky according to specific glue manufactures instructions, usually two to five minutes.

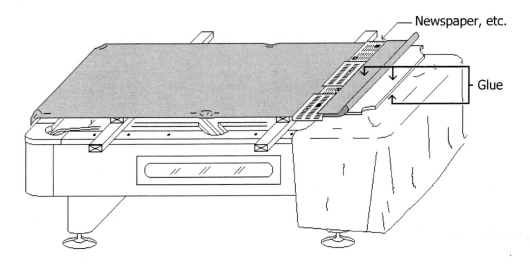

Newspaper, etc.

Glue

Figure 17-23 *Apply glue to slate and underside of cloth*

Unfold and attach the *middle* of the bed cloth to the top and edge of the slate, letting the cloth end overhang, but do not attach the bottom at this time. Stretch the cloth toward each side of that end of the slate and attach, keeping the cloth edge parallel with the edge of the slate. From the bottom of the slate, at the pocket cutouts, cut the overhanging cloth at a 45-degree angle down and in (Figure 17-24). This prevents the excess from

Caution

Some manufacturers and mechanics glue only the top and edge, while others glue only the bottom and edge. However, it will not harm the table to glue all three surfaces—top, edge, and bottom—to insure that the cloth holds.

wrapping into the pocket cutout when it is folded under and attached.

After cutting the angle, fold the overhanging cloth under the slate and attach it to the bottom, but do not allow the cloth to pucker or crease beneath the slate; it must be smooth so the slate can set flat within the frame (Figure 17-24).

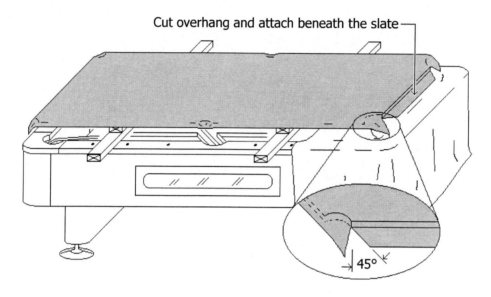

Cut overhang and attach beneath the slate

45°

Figure 17-24 *Attach first end*

Glue and Attach Second End

Protect the other end of the table with a drop cloth or old bed cloth, and fold 8 to 10 inches of that end of the bed cloth over so the underside shows. Apply glue in the same manner as the first end-edges of slate, approximately 2 inches on top and bottom, and approximately 4 inches along the width of the underside of the cloth.

After the glue has become tacky, stretch the middle as tight as possible

Caution

Pliers make stretching easier, but can also rip the cloth. Use them with discretion.

to that end and attach the top and edge (Figure 17-25). Do not let up while attaching. Cloth will begin to loosen almost immediately, and over time can become very loose.

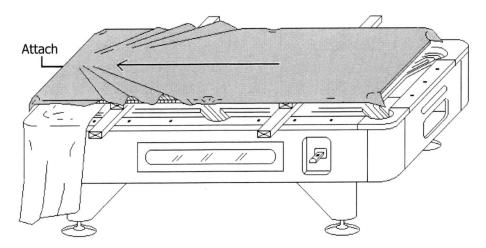

Figure 17-25 *Stretch center and attach*

Next, stretch the cloth toward the sides of that end, pulling parallel with the side of the slate and from the opposite end of the table, and attach to the top and edge of the slate. Again, stretch as tight as possible while attaching to the top and edge of the slate (Figure 17-26).

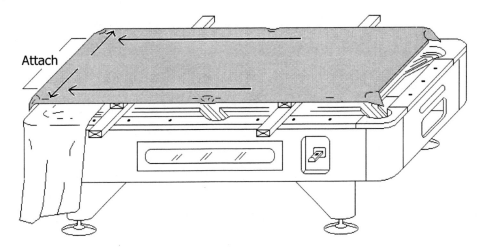

Figure 17-26 *Stretch parallel with slate and attach*

As before, cut the overhanging cloth at a 45-degree angle from the pocket cutouts before attaching beneath the slate (refer back to Figure 17-24), and as before, do not let the cloth pucker or crease beneath the slate.

Glue and Attach One Side

Protect one side of the table with a drop cloth or old bed cloth. Fold 6 to 8 inches of cloth of that side over the slate exposing the underside. Apply glue to the slate and the underside of the cloth as before. This time include the pocket cutouts in the gluing process (Figure 17-27). Use newspaper, cardboard, etc. to protect the top of the cloth.

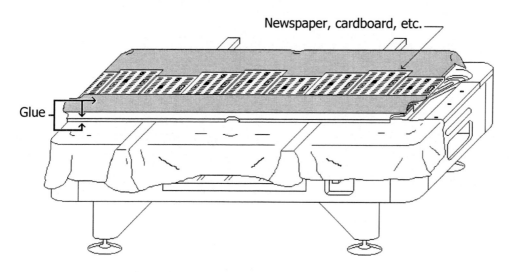

Figure 17-27 *Apply glue to slate and cloth*

Unfold the cloth and stretch it along that side of the slate, from the center pocket cutout toward the corner pocket cutouts, and attach the ends, next to the corner pocket cutouts—top and edge only. Allow the cloth to pucker slightly in the corner pocket cutouts. Attach the remainder of that side, keeping the edge of the cloth parallel with the slate.

Cut the overhang at a 45-degree angle from the pocket cutouts then attach to the bottom of the slate (Figure 17-28).

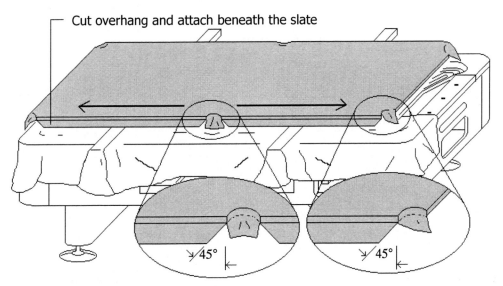

Figure 17-28 *Attach first side*

Glue and Attach Second Side

Glue the other side (do not forget the drop cloth, etc.), and stretch the bed cloth along that side, first one end, and then the other. This time, however, pull the cloth from across the slate at the same time. Stretch it as tight as possible, try to get a slight pucker in the corner pocket cutouts, and attach the top and edges only (Figure 17-29).

Most of the cloth will pull from across the slate. Cut the overhang at a 45-degree angle from the pocket cutouts and attach to the bottom of the slate.

Cut overhang and attach beneath the slate

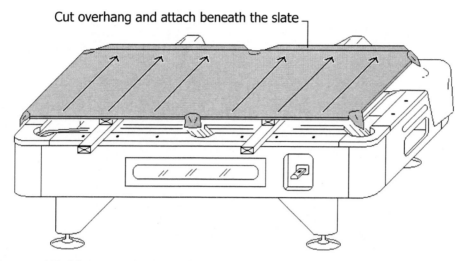

Figure 17-29 *Attach the other side*

Glue and Attach Pocket Cutouts

To finish, slit the cloth in the pocket cutouts to make four to six tabs depending on the curvature of the cutout—the smaller the radius the more tabs. Try to prevent the slits from extending up past the bottom of the slate. If they do, keep them to within a quarter to a half the thickness of the slate.

Trick of the Trade

Strapping tape on the bottom surface of the slate, across all of the tabs, will help prevent them from slipping.

The use of pocket cutout padding (see Figure 17-1) up to half the thickness of the slate may be used behind the tabs to hide the slate and, if used, should be installed before the tabs are attached. Please note, though, that the gluing surface used for the padding could be crucial in holding the tabs in place. This padding is, therefore, not shown in Figures 17-30 or 17-31, nor recommended for coin-operated, one-piece slate tables.

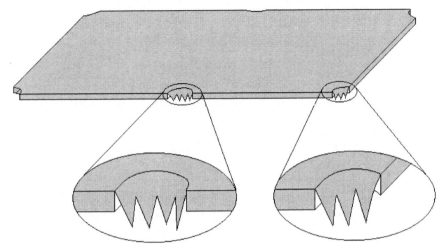

Figure 17-30 *Cut pocket cutout tabs*

And, finally, pull each tab tight and attach to the slate edge and bottom (Figure 17-31).

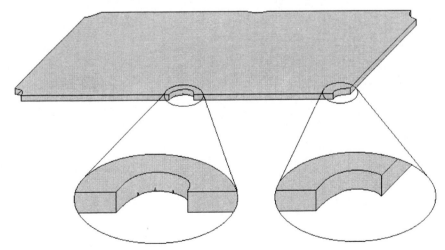

Figure 17-31 *Attach tabs to slate*

NON-REGULATION TABLES

Some non-regulation tables are, in some form or another, combinations of the tables discussed above, but it do not meet some specific requirement to be considered regulation.

Most non-regulation tables, though, are non-slate tables. These kinds of tables generally use particle board (or some other composite board) for the playing surface. The bed cloth can be stapled, tacked, or glued, although glue is usually the preferred method. Cloth should be attached to any man-made or manufactured playing surface according to the manufacturer's recommendations.

On The Level

I once re-covered a non-slate table that was so warped that the cloth didn't touch the center of the playing surface The ball actually furrowed the fabric as is rolled.

When recovering a non-regulation table, follow the procedures for a regulation **backed** table if the cloth is to be stapled, or for a regulation **unbacked** or coin-operated table if the cloth is to be glued. Some manufacturers glue the entire bed cloth onto the bed of non-slate tables. If so, the cloth must be peeled away and the bed scraped as much as possible. When it is replaced, however, the new cloth should only be attached at the edge of the bed.

RAIL CLOTH

Whether re-covering and existing pool table or assembling a new one, most people, including some pool table mechanics, consider the installation of rail cloth to be more difficult than the installation of bed cloth, but this is not necessarily the case. The ensuing instructions are straightforward and easy to follow and, if followed, anyone can do a professional looking job.

An ideal workbench, with vises, clamps, and handy tool racks is nice, but it is not always easy to come up with, nor is it particularly necessary. Although not ideal, there is nothing wrong with using the pool table bed as a workbench. Simply spread a drop cloth or an old bed cloth across the top of the slate to protect the rails from scratches and dings, arrange all needed tools within easy reach, and go to work.

FLAT RAILS AND T-RAILS

Remove Old Rail Cloth

To remove the old cloth, lay the rail upside down on the work surface and pull all tacks or staples that hold the rail cloth to the tacking strip, including those around the edges of the cushion facings.

Next, turn the rail right side up to expose the feather strip (Figure 18-1). **It is not necessary to remove the facing as shown in Figure 18-1**.

(Although the following drawings show a flat rail, T-rails are handled in the same manner. Also, some flat rails are uni-constructed; that is, all six rails are made as one unit. In this case, remove all staples of all six rails before turning the unit right side up.)

Feather Strips

Brush dirt and chalk dust from the feather strip. Often nails or staples have been used to wedge loose feather strips into place. If any are present, use a tack puller to remove them. Take care not to scar the top rail. Also, some feather strips may be covered with masking or strapping tape. Tape is used to smooth the rough edges of high feather strips. If present, tape must be removed.

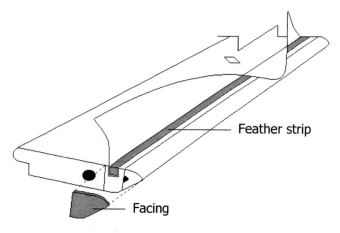

Figure 18-1 *Expose feather strip*

To extract the feather strip, start at one end of the rail and pull straight up on the old rail cloth, pulling it and the feather strip out simultaneously (Figure 18-2).

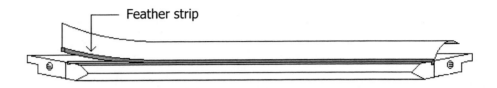

Figure 18-2 *Remove feather strip*

Feather strips that are tight and difficult can be removed with a long, thin blade screwdriver. Start at one end, behind a facing, and carefully drive the screwdriver below the feather strip, at the bottom of the rail grove (Figure 18-3). Be careful not to mar or chip the laminate of the top rail, and try not to break the feather strip.

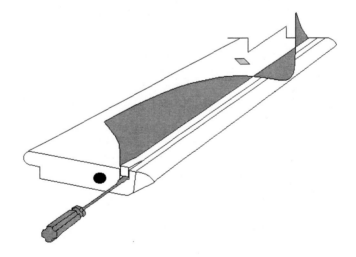

Figure 18-3 *Difficult feather strip*

Unbroken feather strips can be reused. More often than not, they fit better than new ones that have to be trimmed. Reusing broken feather strips is also possible if there are few pieces, or if the pieces are not too small. However, feather strips that are badly cracked, splintered, or chipped should be replaced.

New Feather Strips

Wooden feather strips are shipped long and need to be cut to their proper length. Lay them in their respective rail groove and mark the facing angle on each end then cut them at that angle, a utility knife or small hacksaw works fine (Figure 18-4). A double cloth thickness clearance should be left between the facings and the end of the feather strip. Feather strips cut too long will bulge into the pocket opening, and those cut too short may allow the cloth to wrinkle at the top rail.

Caution

Thin or loose top rail laminates often break or chip as the rail cloth is removed, so go slow and easy.

Plastic feather strips often come in one long coil. Using a utility knife cut the coil into six equal strips; each strip should be longer than the rails. Because they will stretch, they should be trimmed as they are being installed.

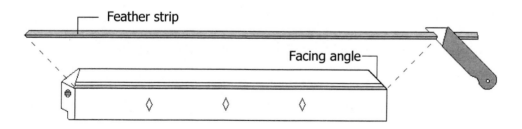

Feather strip

Facing angle

Figure 18-4 *Cut the feather strips to fit.*

Allow approximately one-half cloth thickness for clearance on each side of the grove (one thickness overall), and one-half cloth thickness at the bottom (Figure 18-5). Tighten loose (thin) feather strips by wrapping them with masking tape or doubling the rail cloth. This is far better than wedging them in with nails or staples.

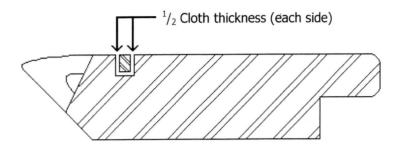

Figure 18-5 *Normal feather strip clearance*

Wood and some hard plastic feather strips that are too tight (thick) can be shaved with a small wood plane or file, or they can be sized by simply eliminating the front space, allowing only one-half cloth thickness at the back. This works fine as long as the feather strip fits snuggly (Figure 18-6).

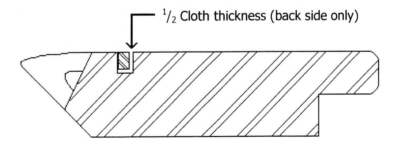

Figure 18-6 *Wide feather strip clearance*

Although this clearance does not have to be precise, it should be close. (For reference: 21/22-ounce cloth is approximately .032 of an inch thick.) Calipers can be used to obtain the exact thickness of the feather strip, or simply use a scrap piece of cloth to get a "feel" for how tight it is going to be.

Using a rubber mallet, a feather strip should drive in smoothly and with relative ease, but must have some resistance. If it can be inserted without being driven, it is too loose, which will allow the cloth to pull away. If it is too tight and must be driven with vigor, it could force the grove open, weakening or cracking the rail.

Stiff plastic feather strips are usually made hollow so if they are a little tight they will collapse as they are being driven in. Flexible plastic feather strips that are too loose should not be used, but if they are a little too tight, they can be stretched to fit as they are being driven in.

"A little tight" and "a little loose" are judgment phrases that common sense should dictate. A good rule-of-thumb is a cloth thickness clearance of zero is too tight, one cloth thickness is perfect, and anything greater is probably too loose.

After the feather strips have been prepared, insert and center each into its prospective grove. Draw a line across the center of each feather strip and rail, toward the cushion, to show their relative positions (Figure 18-7).

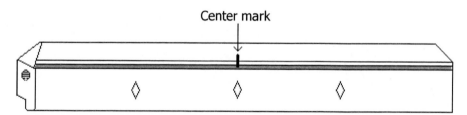

Figure 18-7 *Center mark feather strip*

This mark will insure that the feather strip can be returned to its original or centered location during the re-cover process. If the feather strip is in more than one piece, mark each piece.

The order in which rails are covered is unimportant, but it is generally easier to start with the end rails.

End rails and side rails differ in the way the pocket angles are cut. End rails have two corner pocket angles and side rails have one corner pocket angle and one center pocket angle. The angle of the corner pocket is cut wider (Figure 18-8). These angles are treated differently in the covering process. The cloth is pulled over the facing of the corner pocket angle and folded over the center pocket angle.

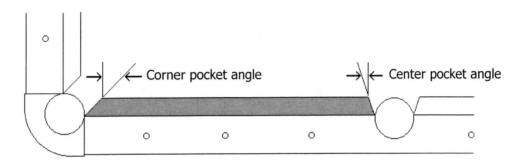

Figure 18-8 *Rail angle cuts*

End Rails

Lay the rail cloth *face down* on top of the top rail (remember that the cloth is folded face in and the back should be marked). Depending on how tight the feather strip is, extend one long edge of the rail cloth zero to $^1/_2$ inch over the feather strip grove, and allow both ends to overhang the rail two or more inches (direc-tional cloth should lie smooth right to left so the nap will run clockwise around the pool table).

Place the feather strip above the cloth and grove, and align the marks (rail 1 in Figure 18-9).

Gently drive the *center* of the feather strip a quarter to half way into the grove with a rubber mallet (rail 2 in Figure 18-9).

Now, stretch one end of the cloth toward its end of the rail, maintaining the zero to $^1/_2$-inch extension over the grove. At the same time, using a rubber mallet, drive the feather strip a quarter to half way into the grove. (If the feather strip is flexible plastic, stretch it along with the cloth.) Continue this until within approximately 3 inches of the end.

If you are using plastic feather strips, they will stretch past the ends of the rails. Mark the facing angles and cut them at that angle before continuing. Wooden feather strips will not stretch.

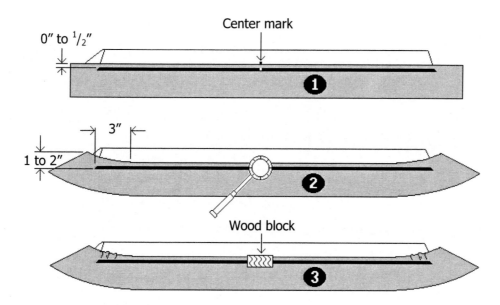

Figure 18-9 *Seating feather strip on end rail*

From that 3-inch point, pull 1 to 2 inches of cloth from beneath the feather strip, toward the cushion, making a triangular shape of approximately 3 x $1^1/_2$ inches (rail 2 in Figure 18-9). Keeping the cloth taut, drive in the remaining section of feather strip a quarter to half way into the grove.

Repeat the process for the other end of the rail.

Then, using a block of wood and a rubber mallet, drive the feather strip until tight or flush with the top rail (rail 3 in Figure 18-9). Keep the wood block flat and level so the feather strip will seat uniformly.

Side Rails

Place and seat the feather strip the same as an end rail, including the triangle at the corner pocket end.

But the center pocket end of side rails is dealt with in a slightly different manner. After completing the corner pocket end, pull the cloth straight toward the center pocket angle (rail 2 in Figure 18-10).

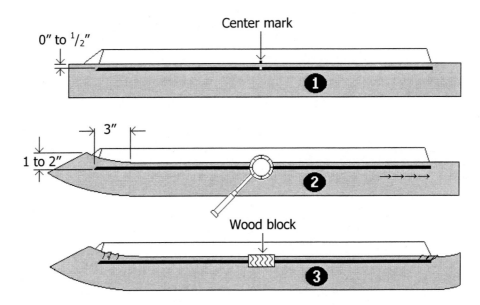

Figure 18-10 *Seating feather strip on side rail*

Using a block of wood and a rubber mallet, drive the feather strip until tight or flush with the top rail (rail 3 in Figure 18-10). Keep the wood block flat and level so the feather strip will seat uniformly.

End and Side Rails

On the cushion side, carefully trim the excess cloth flush with the top of the feather strip, if there is any (Figure 18-11). Do not allow the knife to slice the cloth on the top rail side of the feather strip.

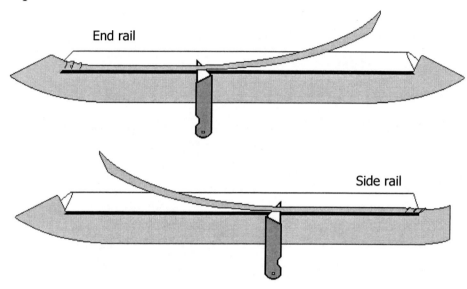

End rail

Side rail

Figure 18-11 *Trim excess cloth*

Using the block of wood and the rubber mallet, seat the feather strip flush with the top of the rail, leaving approximately one cloth thickness above the top rail, but don't drive it below the rim of the grove. A piece of scrap cloth between the wood block and the top rail will prevent top rail damage, and help control feather strip height (Figure 18-12).

If the feather strip goes below the top rail, remove it and shim the bottom of the grove with strips of cloth cut the same width and length of the grove. If the feather strip is profusely higher than the top rail, remove it and trim the bottom. Ideally, one cloth thickness should remain above the top rail.

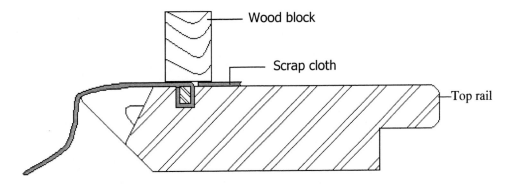

Figure 18-12 *Protect the top rail*

Attaching The Rail Cloth

Next, turn the rail face down and pull the new rail cloth flat beneath it so the cloth lies flat on the work surface (Figure 18-13). Make sure old cloth, nails, staples, and other rubbish have been cleared from between the rail cloth and rail. Also, make sure there are no loose staples or other debris remaining on or around the work area that can scratch the top rail or cut the new cloth.

End Rails

Starting at a corner pocket end, imagine a line running diagonally from the point of the cushion (and facing) to the outside edge of the rail cloth. Also, imagine two more lines running parallel with each edge of the cloth (Figure 18-13).

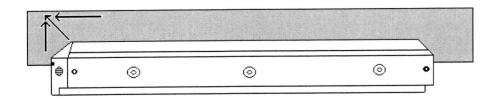

Figure 18-13 *Draw cloth toward its outside corner.*

Where those lines converge at the edge of the cloth, using moderate force, pull the cloth diagonally away from the rail.

Keeping the cloth taut, fold the imaginary lines over the facing, onto the rail bottom, and staple there (Figure 18-14). Pulling the cloth diagonally, as if pulling in three directions at the same time, is important. This helps to eliminate puckers and folds.

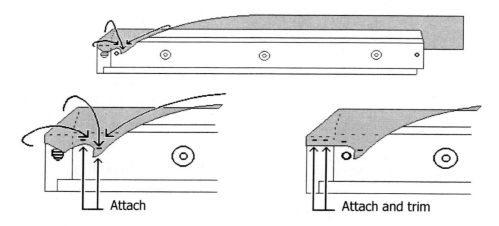

Figure 18-14 *Fold cloth over facing and attach*

Next, pull the cloth smooth across the facing and in little gathers at the bottom of the rail, below the facing. (Remember the rail is upside-down; the bottom of the rail is being worked on.) Drive a staple into each gather, and around the perimeter of the facing, so the cloth is held smooth over the facing. At first, this may seem difficult on a T-rail because of the lack of space for attaching, but, with patience and a little practice, it can be done.

End rails have two corner pocket ends; simply repeat the above procedure for the other end (Figure 18-15).

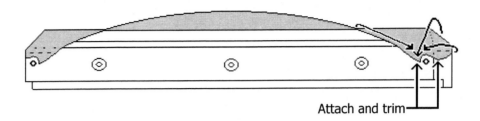

Attach and trim

Figure 18-15 *End rails have two corner pocket ends*

Side Rails

Because side rails have a center pocket end and a corner pocket end, they are treated differently. After following the above procedures for the corner pocket end, pull the cloth in the direction of the center pocket end, wrap it onto the rail bottom, and staple it there (Figure 18-16).

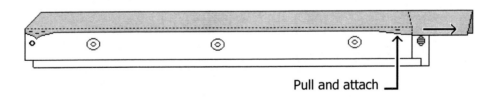

Pull and attach

Figure 18-16 *Side rails have corner and center pocket ends*

To complete the center pocket end, pull the bottom portion of the rail cloth over the facing, and staple it behind the facing (rail 2 in Figure 18-17). This makes two creases, one inside, and one outside. Slice the cloth along the inside crease to within $1/4$ inch of the facing tip to eliminate that crease (rail 3 in Figure 18-17).

Next, keeping the outside crease intact, pull the cloth—and the crease—up and over the facing, onto the bottom of the rail, and staple there. That outside crease should follow the front edge of the facing at the same angle as the cushion (rail 4 in Figure 18-17).

Attach around the back perimeter of the facing while pulling the cloth taut. Do not allow the cloth to pucker on the facing or cushion (rail 5 in Figure 18-17). Trim excess cloth from the back of the facing and bottom of the rail (rail 6 in Figure 18-17).

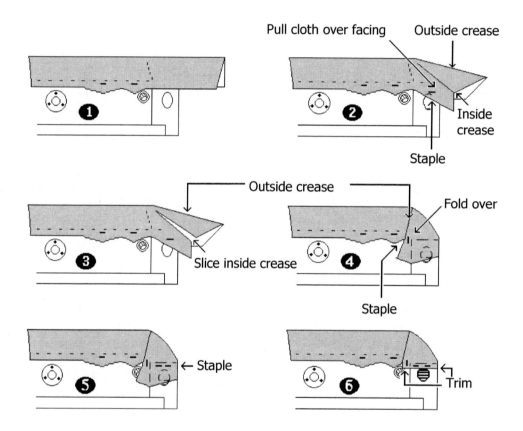

Figure 18-17 *Center pocket fold*

Both End and Side Rails

The following instructions are for both end and side rails. At the midpoint, smoothly pull the rail cloth over the bottom of the rail and staple there (rail 1 in Figure 18-18). *Do not* pull the cloth so tight that it causes an indentation in the cushion nose, and do not let the cloth pucker on the cushion. Continue pulling and stapling at approximately $^1/_2$ to 1 inch increments, pulling slightly away from the end and toward the previous staple, until that end of the rail is reached (rail 2 and 3 in Figure 18-18).

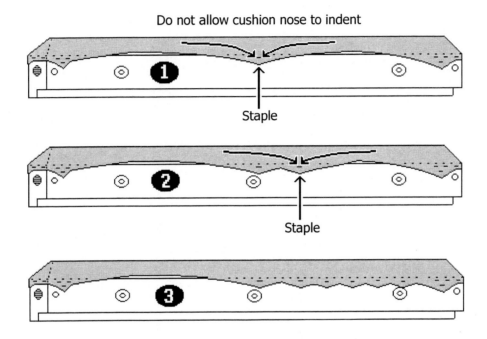

Figure 18-18 *Work from midpoint toward ends*

Some rails have a tacking grove running the length of the bottom of the rail. Try to staple within that grove. Staples outside the grove might change the height of the cushion nose when the rails are installed (see Chapter 19).

Repeat to finish the other end of that rail.

Attaching the cloth at $^1/_2$ to 1 inch intervals will usually suffice. However, insert the staples as close to each other as necessary to prevent wrinkling in the rail cloth on any exposed part of the rail. If puckers

Trick of the Trade

Pliers can be used to hold and pull the rail cloth; however, they tend to indent the cushion nose inordinately. Use caution

occur put a staple in each pucker, so they stay on the bottom of the rail.

Finally, trim all excess cloth from the rail. Trim close to the staples to eliminate the possibility of the cloth wrinkling or folding under the rail when it is installed (Figure 18-19).

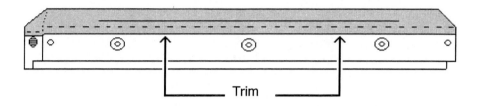

Figure 18-19 *Trim excess cloth*

CAROM, SNOOKER, AND REBOUND TABLES

Carom, snooker, and rebound table rails are covered in the same manner as pool table rails with these two exceptions:

(1) Carom and rebound tables have no pockets and, therefore, no facings. The cloth can be pulled around the rail ends like coin-operated rails as shown in "Detachable rails (Coin-operated Tables)" later in this Chapter. Or, the cloth can be cut and stapled within the rail ends where they are mitered together.

(2) Snooker tables have cushions that are rounded into each pocket, including the side rails. The cloth must be pulled and stretched around all rail ends as if each were an end rail. There are *no* center pocket folds like those shown in "Flat Rails and T-rails" at the beginning of this chapter.

COIN-OPERATED-TABLES

The side rails of coin-operated tables differ from end rails in the cut of the facing angles, exactly like flat rails and T-rails differ. However, unlike other rails, it is customary to eliminate the fold at the center pocket angle by pulling the cloth smooth around the facing as if it were a corner pocket angle. Though somewhat troublesome, this method of covering coin-operated table rails is efficient and clean-looking when finished. So, if it proves to be difficult, coin-operated table rails can be covered following the procedures for non-coin-operated tables; see "Non-Coin-Operated Tables" later in this chapter.

Before re-covering previously covered coin-operated rails, all staples, tacks, and old rail cloth must be removed from the rails. Make sure all debris has been cleared from around the work area. Old staples and nails can cut the new cloth.

To protect the new rail cloth, spread an old bed cloth or some similar padding across the slate (or workbench).

The order in which rails are covered is of no importance.

Begin by laying the rail cloth *face down* on the work area, and placing the rail on it, with the cushion nose down (rail 1 in Figure 18-20). (Directional cloth should lie smooth right to left, so the nap will run clockwise around the table.) Center the rail end-to-end, but position the top of the rail approximately $2/3$ of the way down from the upper (top) edge of the cloth.

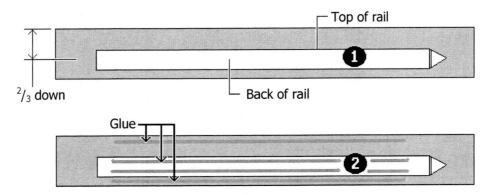

Figure 18-20 *Position rail on cloth, and apply glue*

The top and bottom edges of the cloth can be either stapled or glued to the back of the rail, but the ends must be stapled. If the cloth is to be glued, apply the glue at this time. Use a spray adhesive like 3M brand 76 or 77, or contact cement. Apply glue to the back of the rail and an inch or so along the top and bottom edges of the cloth (rail 2 in Figure 18-20).

Whether stapled or glued, fold one end of the cloth over that end of the rail and staple about 1 inch from the end (rail 2 in Figure 18-21).

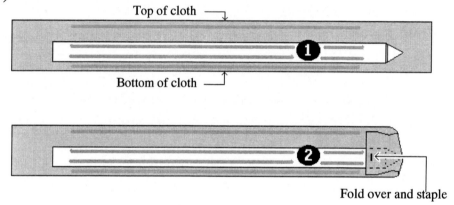

Figure 18-21 *Fold one end and staple*

Next, stretch the cloth beneath the rail from the stapled end to the other end (rail 1 in Figure 18-22). Pull very tight using one hand on the cloth and the other on the rail. Fold that end of the cloth over that end of the rail and staple about 1 inch from the end of the rail (rail 2 in Figure 18-22). Trim the excess cloth (rail 3 in Figure 18-22).

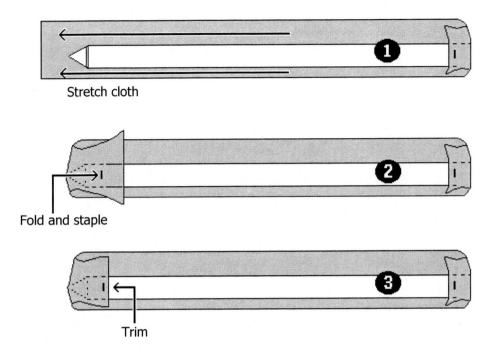

Figure 18-22 *Fold second end, attach and trim*

Now, fold the top corners of the cloth over the top edge of the rail, to the back, and staple it there (rail 1 in Figure 18-23

Trim excess cloth close to the staples (rail 2 in Figure 18-23

Next, fold the bottom corners over the bottom edge of the rail, staple to the back, and trim excess cloth from those corners (rail 3 in Figure 18-23

These corners must be pulled tight and in small gathers at the back of the rail. At least one staple should go into each gather. Do not let the cloth pucker or ripple on any rail surface that will be exposed when installed.

Again, even if gluing, the ends of the rails must be stapled as shown.

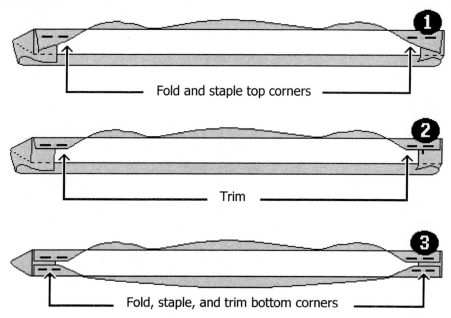

Figure 18-23 *Fold, staple ends, and trim*

Glued Rails

Fold the top of the cloth onto the back of the rail, pulling slightly toward the center, simultaneously attaching the cloth along the back of the rail. If glue was applied earlier, it should be tacky at this time and will hold simply by pressing the cloth to the rail back (rail 1 in Figure 18-24).

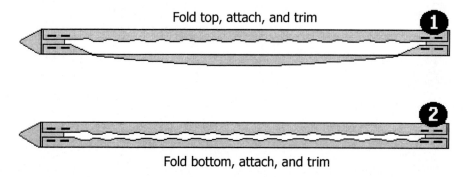

Figure 18-24 *Glue the edges of the cloth to the back of the rail*

Glued cloth can be repositioned a couple of times to insure a smooth job. If any part puckers or does not hold simply drive a staple in that area.

Turn the rail over and repeat the process for the bottom: fold the bottom of the cloth onto the back of the rail while pulling slightly toward the center and attaching along the back of the rail (rail 2 in Figure 18-24).

When pulling the cloth over the bottom of the rail, it must be pulled hard enough to stretch across the cushion without leaving wrinkles, but *do not* pull it so tight that it causes indentations in the cushion nose.

Trim any excess cloth that covers the rail bolt holes.

Stapled Rails

Fold the top of the cloth onto the back of the rail, pulling slightly toward the center, and simultaneously stapling along the back (rail 1 in Figure 18-25. Make sure all puckers are pulled to the back of the rail and stapled.

Turn the rail over and repeat the process for the bottom: fold the bottom of the cloth onto the back of the rail while pulling slightly toward the center and stapling along the back of the rail (rail 2 in Figure 18-25).

Trim any excess cloth that covers the rail bolt holes.

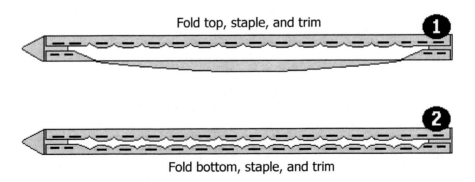

Fold top, staple, and trim **1**

Fold bottom, staple, and trim **2**

Figure 18-25 *Staple the edges of the cloth to the back of the rails*

When pulling the cloth over the bottom, it must be pulled hard enough to stretch across the cushion without leaving wrinkles, but *do not* pull it so tight that it causes indentations in the cushion nose.

NON COIN-OPERATED TABLES

Non coin-operated table rails differ slightly from coin-operated rails in that the cloth is *not* pulled over both pocket angles. Therefore, they must be covered in a way similar to flat rails; that is, with a fold over the facings at the center pocket angle. There are two reasons for this. One, stretching the cloth over the center pocket angle (without folds) can be difficult and frustrating, and two, some detachable rails are too wide to allow for stretching without folds. In these cases using the following instructions are simple and efficient.

Before recovering non-coin-operated detachable rails, all staples, tacks, and old rail cloth must be removed from the rails. The order in which rails are covered is unimportant, but it is generally easier to start with the end rails because both facings are corner angles and less difficult to cover. To protect the new rail cloth, spread the old bed cloth or some similar padding across the table (or workbench).

End Rails

To begin, lay the rail right side up on the work area, with the cushion nose facing away. Place the rail cloth *face up* over the top of the rail so approximately $1/2$ inch will fold over the back. Allow both ends of the cloth to overhang the rail 2 or more inches. Attach the folded $1/2$ inch of cloth to the back of the rail by first driving a staple at the midpoint. Then gently stretch the cloth toward one end and staple every inch or so toward that end, to a point approximately 3 inches from the end (rail 1 in Figure 18-26).

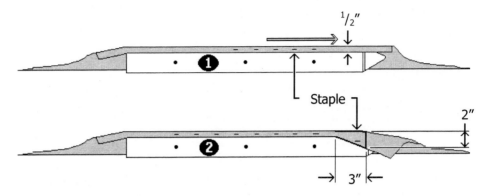

Figure 18-26 *Staple cloth to the top part of the back of the rail*

From that point, pull the cloth down the back side of the rail a couple of inches to form a triangular shape of approximately 3 x 2 inches, and staple (rail 2 in Figure 18-26).

Repeat this process for the other end of the rail.

Next, turn the rail over, topside down, and pull the new cloth flat beneath it (Figure 18-27). Make sure old cloth, nails, staples, and debris have been cleared from between the rail cloth and rail. Do not allow loose staples to remain on or around the work area, because they can cut the new cloth.

Starting at a corner pocket end (either end for end rails), imagine a line running diagonally from the point of the cushion (and facing) to the outside edge of the rail cloth. Also, imagine two more lines, one running parallel with each edge of the cloth (Figure 18-27).

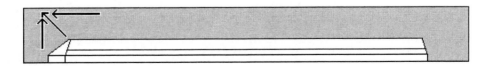

Figure 18-27 *Pull cloth toward corner*

Where those lines converge at the edge of the cloth, using moderate force, pull the cloth diagonally away from the rail. Keeping the cloth taut, fold the imaginary lines over the facing onto the rail bottom and staple there (rail 1 in Figure 18-28). Pulling the cloth diagonally, as if pulling in three directions at the same time helps to eliminate puckers and wrinkles.

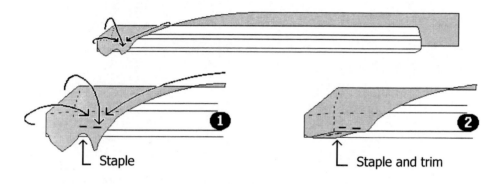

Figure 18-28 *Pull cloth over facing and attach*

Now, pull the cloth smooth across the facing, forcing any gathers to the bottom of the rail, below the facing. (Remember the rail is upside-down.) Drive a staple into each gather, at the bottom of the rail, and several around the perimeter of the facing, so the cloth will be held smooth over the facing.

Trim the excess cloth from around the facing, close to the staples (rail 2 in Figure 18-28).

End rails have two corner pocket angles, so simply repeat the above procedure for the other end (Figure 18-29).

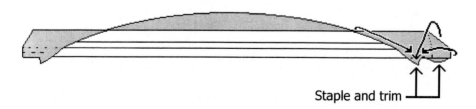

Figure 18-29 *End rails have two corner pocket angles*

Side Rails

Side rails have one corner pocket angle and one center pocket angle. **After following the above procedures for the corner pocket angle**, pull the cloth toward the center pocket angle, wrap it onto the rail bottom, and staple there (Figure 18-30)

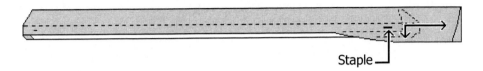

Staple

Figure 18-30 *Pull cloth toward center pocket angle, and staple*

To complete the center pocket angle of a side rail, pull the rail cloth that covers the bottom of the cushion over the facing, toward the back, and staple behind the facing. This makes two natural creases, one inside, and one outside. Slice the cloth along the inside crease to within $^1/_4$ inch of the facing tip to eliminate that crease (rail 1 in Figure 18-31).

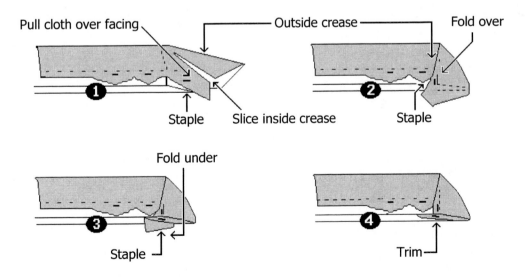

Figure 18-31 *Center pocket(side rail) angle fold*

Keeping the outside crease intact, pull the cloth (and the crease) up and over the facing, fold it onto the bottom of the rail, and staple there. That outside crease should follow the front edge of the facing at the same angle as the bottom of the cushion (rail 2 in Figure 18-31).

Staple around the back perimeter of the facing while pulling the cloth taut (rail 3 in Figure 18-31), and do not allow the cloth to pucker on the facing or cushion.

Trim the excess cloth from around the facing close to the staples (rail 4 in Figure 18-31).

Both End and Side Rails

The following instructions are for both end and side rails. At the midpoint, smoothly pull the rail cloth over the rail to the bottom (or back) and staple (rail 1 in Figure 18-32).

Do not pull the cloth so tight that it causes an indentation in the cushion nose, and do not let the cloth pucker or wrinkle on any part of the cushion that will show. Continue pulling and stapling at approximately $^1/_2$ to 1 inch increments, stretching slightly from the end toward the last staple, until that end is reached (rails 2 and 3 in Figure 18-32). **Repeat to finish the other end.**

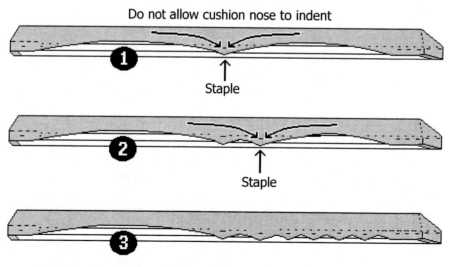

Figure 18-30 *Work from midpoint*

Stapling the cloth at $^1/_2$ to 1 inch intervals will usually suffice. However, insert the staples as close to each other as necessary to prevent the rail cloth from puckering on any part of the rail that will be exposed once installed. If puckers occur on the back or bottom of the rail, put a staple in each so they stay put.

Trick of the Trade

Pliers can be used to hold and pull the rail cloth; however, they tend to indent the cushion nose inordinately. Use caution

Finally, trim all excess cloth from the rail, and trim close to the staples to eliminate the possibility of cloth folds under or behind the rail when it is installed on the table (Figure 18-33).

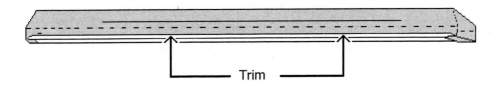

Trim

Figure 18-33 *Trim excess cloth*

WORDS OF EXPERIENCE

Years ago, I drove a small Toyota pickup on which I installed runners on top of the camper shell that worked and looked much like a construction worker's ladder rack. I could heave a unibody table across the rack, tie it down, and be off, negating the remotest possibility of any auto insurance company covering me.

On a beautiful Arizona winter afternoon, while driving along the canal on Camelback Road just east of Scottsdale, I heard an odd thud. Looking back, I could see the table was still there, but I stopped anyway. A new Mercedes SL450 convertible pulled in behind me.

The driver—middle age, well-trimmed moustache, expensive suit, driving gloves—stepped out. He looked like Mr. Money himself. "You're right," he said, "you lost something." He held up the side door of the coin-op table I was hauling.

"Excuse me?" I asked as if I misunderstood.

"It hit the windshield," Mr. Money said. "It skipped over my head and landed in the back seat."

"I'm terribly sorry," I managed. "But—"

"Look," Mr. Money very coolly interrupted, "you put new cushions on my snooker table a few months ago. You had to plane the rails down because they were manufactured too high for a snooker table to begin with. I appreciate the fine job you did for me. The table has never played better."

"Oh, yes, Doctor Vandenburg. I remember you . . . now."

"Well," he said, "since I don't see any damage other than the windshield, I'll just turn it into the insurance company as road damage and let them fix it." He handed me the door, climbed back into his Mercedes, and drove off.

I've recovered his table twice since.

If you do the best work you can do, on every job, it'll pay dividends.

Thanks Doc.

216

CUSHIONS

Installing cushions, although time consuming, is not expensive or difficult.

Cushions usually deteriorate slowly, and noticing the gradual loss of resiliency of the rubber is impossible while using a particular table exclusively. Cushions can last thirty years or more and still be playable. Normally, however, they should be replaced every five or six years or whenever they fail to rebound properly.

Some cushions become hard as they age and others will soften, and feeling or squeezing them will not necessarily give a good indication of their playability. A better way is to swiftly roll a ball against a rail. The ball should rebound back and forth from four to six times; that is, three on the first side and two or three on the other side (Figure 19-1).

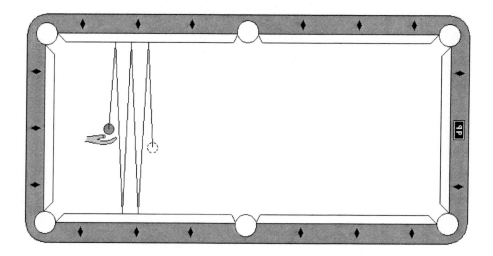

Figure 19-1 *Five rebounds*

Although 100 percent gum rubber cushions are considered regulation, many tables are manufactured using a variety of synthetics or extruded rubbers, and replacements might be difficult to find. However, all cushion rubber is installed in the same manner, so the following instructions can be used to replace any of them.

POOL TABLES

All figurers in this section depict flat rails. However, cushion rubber on T-rails and detachable (including coin-operated table) rails are installed the same in the same way.

To begin, spread the old bed cloth, or other protective covering, on top of the pool table or workbench to prevent damaging the top rails or slate.

Lay a side rail right side up onto the work area. Notice that the ends of the old cushions have been cut at an angle to form the pocket "facings." Also, notice that the corner pocket facing angles are greater than the center pocket facing angles (Figure 19-2).

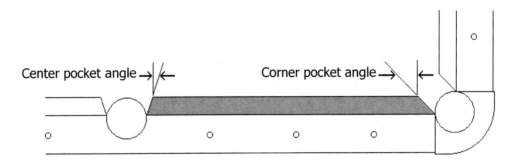

Figure 19-2 *Rail pocket angles*

These angles must be transferred to the new rubber. This is done by using a protractor to note the degrees of the angles, or by using two T-bevels. Set one at the corner pocket facing angle, and the other at the center pocket-facing angle (Figure 19-3).

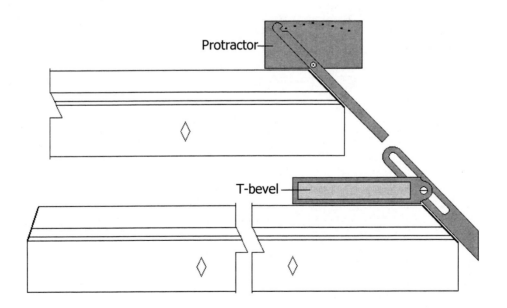

Figure 19-3 *Set or note pocket cutout angles*

The T-bevel (or a protector that has a blade lock) is the preferred tool because once set it stays at its established position, and the mechanic does not have to be concerned with the actual degree of the angles.

If a protractor is used, the degree of the angles should be in close agreement with the specifications in Part I, but do not be alarmed if they differ somewhat. Manufacturers establish their own pocket openings, so each table will vary slightly. However, to maintain a regulation (BCA) opening, it must fall within the limits set in Part I. In normal cases, though, the pocket angle need only be transferred, not changed.

Usually, part of the wood of the rail itself has also been cut at the same angle as the facing and will be used later to align the T-bevel to mark the angle on the new cushion. If the wood has not been cut at an angle, use the edge of the rail. In such a case, setting the T-bevel before the cushions are removed is imperative.

It is only necessary to measure one side rail to establish the angles for all corner and center pocket facings. This also insures that all facings on all rails are cut the same.

In addition, notice that the pocket facing may also slant down, into the rail. This slanting, whether it is small or severe, will be marked on the new rubber for cutting *after* the rubber has been installed. Other than knowing of the slant's existence, it should not be of concern at this time (Figure 19-4).

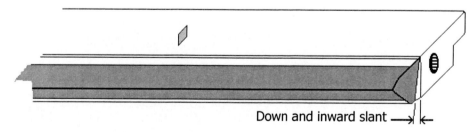

Down and inward slant ⟶

Figure 19-4 *Facing or end rail slant*

Remove Facings

Once the facing angles have been set on the T-bevels (or noted if a protractor is used), detach the facing material from each end of the rail (rail 1 in Figure 19-5). This can be done by inserting a screwdriver to loosen a corner then pulling the facing away. Generally, these facings are reusable. If not, new facings should come with a new set of cushions, or they can be purchased separately.

Remove Old Cushions

After the facings have been removed, slide a screwdriver into the hole created by the recoil space at the back of the cushion and pull it from the rail-gluing surface (rail 2 in Figure 19-5). Some cushions are solid, without the recoil space. In such a case, use a flat blade screwdriver or a knife.

Also, it's important not to peel or splinter the wood beneath the cushion. If it begins to splinter, simply use a sharp utility knife and cut the cushion from the rail. Use wood glue and clamps to reattach large splinters. Fill splits, splinter cavities, and other holes with wood putty.

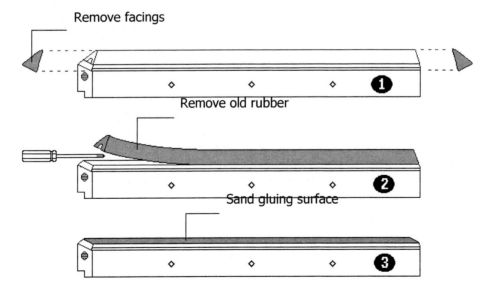

Figure 19-5 *Remove old cushions*

Caution

It is possible to glue the cushions on upside down, so use caution.

Next, sand all rail gluing surfaces smooth (rail 3 in Figure 19-5). A sanding block with course sandpaper is ideal for this purpose. Belt sanders also work fine if care is taken not to alter the angle of the surface or leave concave or scalloped areas. Sanding down to the bare wood is not necessary, providing the gluing surface is smooth and free of old rubber and canvas backing.

Install New Cushions

Clean dust, loose rubber, and old cloth from the rails and work area. Although each rail can be re-cushioned individually, doing all six at the same time saves considerable time.

The back of the cushions will be glued to the rail-gluing surface. Most full profile cushions have canvas vulcanized to the top and back. The top is rounded, and the back has a recoil space that runs its length. The bottom is flat (Figure 19-6).

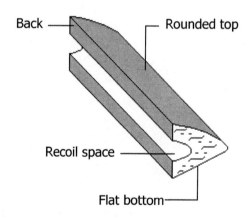

Figure 19-6 *Cushion with canvas*

During manufacturing, the gluing surface of the rail is cut at an angle to insure that the cushion nose will be positioned at the proper height. New cushions can usually be installed at that height by simply aligning the top of the rubber with the top of the rail during application (Figure 19-7).

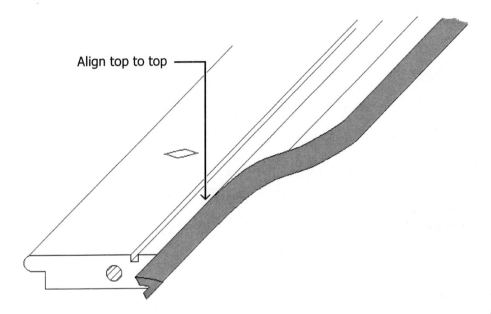

Align top to top

Figure 19-7 *Align tops of rail and cushion*

To begin, brush the back of each cushion and the gluing surface of each rail with quality contact cement (rail 1 in Figure 19-8). Some manufactures will argue for stronger, more resilient glue, but contact cement works fine if allowed to dry and cure properly.

Because contact cement must be applied to both surfaces and allowed to dry before bonding, it becomes time effective to apply the cement on all six cushions and all six rails before attaching any of them.

Allow the cement to dry until it becomes tacky. This usually takes ten to twenty minutes. Nevertheless, the contact cement will remain workable for a few hours so there will be plenty of time.

However, please read the manufacturers instructions on the cement container before starting, some instructions vary slightly.

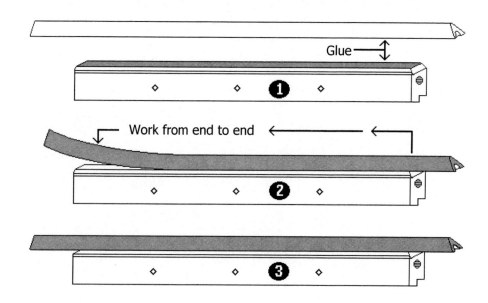

Figure 19-8 *Attach from one end to the other*

Once the cement has become tacky, arrange the first rail on the workbench with the top rail up and glued surface pointing away. Lay the first cushion in front of the rail; top up, glued back pointing to the rail.

Caution

Be aware that once a cushion has made contact with the rail it should not be repositioned without removing and re-gluing.

Begin attaching the cushion at one end. Leave a couple inches of cushion extending past that end of the rail, and align the top of the cushion with the top of the rail to maintain the cushion height, as shown in Figure 1-15. Work to the other end, slightly pulling the cushion as it is being attached (rail 2 in Figure 19-8).

Pulling the cushion slightly will help keep it straight, but, *do not* stretch it. If a cushion is stretched too tight, it will deform slightly, then, after the ends are cut, it could recede back to its original shape, leaving the ends short.

Press the rubber firmly into place, then use a small rubber mallet and moderately strike the cushion nose to set the cement, but do not let the ends vibrate loose.

Cut Cushion Angles

Once the cushions have been attached, retrieve the T-bevel (or protractor) and set its base along the nose of the cushion with the blade crossing the top of the cushion. Align the blade with the pocket-facing angle already cut into the top rail (or with the edge of the top rail if no angle is present, left side of rail 1 in Figure 19-9).

Trick of the Trade

Cushion height can be slightly changed by shimming the rails during installation.

Shimming between the rail and the slate, behind the rail bolts before they are tightened can lower cushions that are too high. Conversely, cushions that are too low can be raised slightly by shimming in front of the rail bolts. This change should not be more than 1/16 of an inch either way (see Chapter 22).

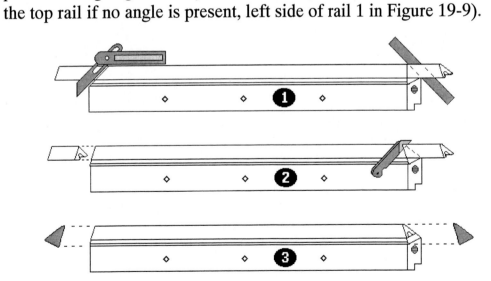

Figure 19-9 *Cut pocket cutout angles*

With a pencil, mark the facing angle on the top of the cushion, from back to nose. Next, hold a small straightedge on the bottom of the cushion, from the bottom edge of the rail up to where it aligns with the line at the nose of the cushion (right side of rail 1 in Figure 19-9). Mark this downward slant of the rail facing. This is the slant shown in Figure 19-4.

Caution

Remember, there are eight corner pocket angles and four center pocket angles.

Using a sharp utility knife cut the rubber along the marked lines. Cut slowly and keep the knife blade at the correct angle and slant (rail 2 in figure 19-9). Follow the lines, and try to keep the cutting as smooth as possible. However, a few slice marks will not hurt anything, and a belt sander with course paper will help smooth the marks, if necessary. Make sure the sander is pulling the cushion into the wood, keeping the bonded surfaces together.

Attach and Trim Facings

After attaching and cutting all six cushions (twelve angles), lay the twelve facings facedown on the work area. Brush a coat of contact cement onto the back of each facing, and onto the angles just cut into cushions and rails. Allow both to dry until tacky, and then attach the facings (Rail 3 in Figure 19-9).

If the facings are new or do not fit properly they must be trimmed flush with the cushion—top and bottom (Figure 19-10).

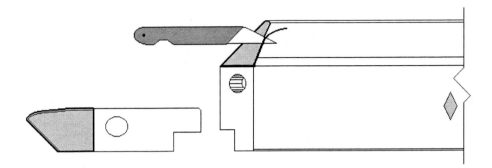

Figure 19-10 *Trim excess facing material*

Facings should be trimmed at a bevel or slightly rounded, do not leave them square or overhanging the cushion.

Finally, using course sandpaper and a sanding block, sand excess rubber, glue, and canvas backing from the joint between the top rail and cushion top. This area should be as smooth as possible so very little of the joint line will be detected once the rail cloth is installed.

Caution

A belt sander works fine for sanding the joint between the rail and cushion. However, use extreme care, do not sand the top rail.

CAROM AND REBOUND TABLES

For carom or rebound tables, follow the proceeding steps for attaching cushions, except there are no pocket cutouts or facings to be dealt with. The cushions are simply cut at the same 45-degree angle as the rails.

SNOOKER TABLES

Snooker cushions differ from pool table cushions in the pocket area. On pool tables, this area is cut flat and covered with a facing material that kills the ball's action as it enters the pocket. Snooker cushions, on the other hand, are rounded into the pockets. This rounding is designed to force a ball to rebound from the pocket if it is not shot perfectly.

Snooker cushions can be installed in one piece; that is, each is attached in the same method as a pool table rail, except the cushion ends are bent around the rail ends, and glued there.

Cut two or three small relief wedges from the back of the cushion to facilitate in the bending and use small nails to secure the cushion ends while the cement cures (rail 1 in Figure 19-11).

Next, roughly trim the bent section of the cushion close to the required radius as shown in rail 2 in Figure 19-11. (See Chapter 2 for radius dimensions.) Use a belt sander with course paper to sand the bends to a more precise radius (rail 3 in Figure 19-11).

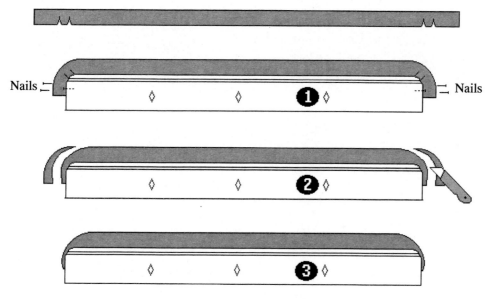

Figure 19-11 *Snooker cushions installed in one piece*

Installing snooker cushions in one piece is not an easy task. Therefore, they are usually installed in three sections: standard cushions in the center and a pre-manufactured "snooker bend" at each end (Figure 19-12).

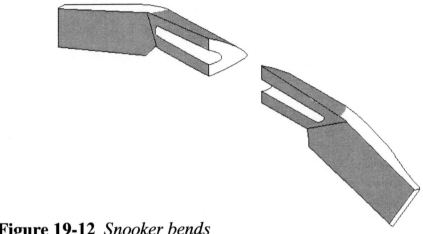

Figure 19-12 *Snooker bends*

The center section of a snooker cushion is attached by following the procedures for a pool table. Each end of the cushion is cut approximately 3 inches short of each end of the rail and a snooker bend is then added to complete the turns (rail 1 in Figure 19-13). The bends and cushion ends must be cut as square as possible and slightly long—no more than $^1/_{16}$ inch—to insure a tight fit. These bends will not make a perfect curve into the pocket any more than did a one-piece cushion. They will also require a couple of nails to hold them in place while the glue sets, and will also have to be trimmed and sanded.

Trick of the Trade

Small spaces or gaps in the joints between the cushion and snooker bends can be filled with a small amount of silicon rubber before sanding.

Snooker bends will also have to be roughly trimmed close to the required radius (rail 2 in Figure 19-13).

The bends can now be sanded to a more precise radius (rail 3 in Figure 19-13). The joints between the cushion and bends can also be sanded to insure a straight and smooth alignment. A belt sander with course grit paper is also ideal for this purpose. (See Chapter 2 for the radius dimensions.)

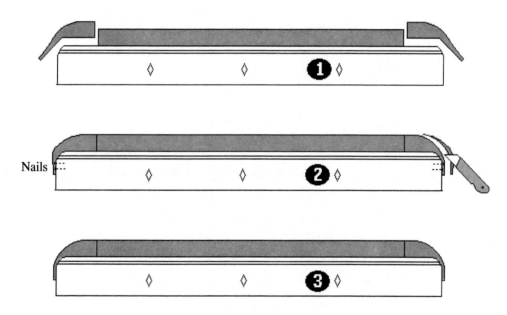

Figure 19-13 *Snooker cushions with snooker bends*

RAILS

Installing rails is relatively straightforward. However, some procedures should be considered in advance to make the job easier. The following instructions give insight into those procedures.

DETACHABLE RAILS

Of the three kinds of rails (detachable, T, and flat), detachable rails are the easiest to install because they are self aligning. Each is screwed directly to its respective top rail, which is essentially a permanent part of the cabinet or frame (Figure 20-1).

To install, set each detachable rail into its relative position around the table. Each position should already be marked or indicated. However, end rails and side rails are different in the way the pocket angles are cut; therefore, the two end rails are generally interchangeable with each other, but they cannot replace a side rail. Side rails are interchangeable on a cater corner basis only (see Chapter 7).

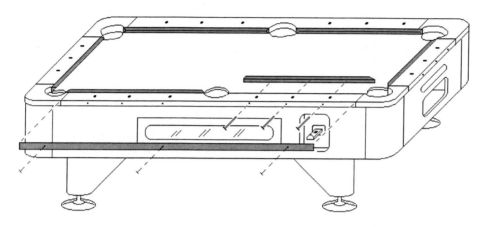

Figure 20-1 *Coin-operated table*

Hold each rail into position and start the rail bolts (or screws), but do not tighten until they are all started. Make sure each end of the rail protrudes equally into its respective pocket area.

To obtain the proper height of the cushion above the playing surface, simply align the top of the detachable rail with the top rail portion of the cabinet. Often this is as easy as holding the rail down against the slate as the bolts are tightened. Double-check the height by measuring the distance from the top of the slate to the nose of the cushion. This distance (approximately $1^7/_{16}$ inches for a standard pool table) should conform to the specification in Chapter 1. Adjustments are not usually necessary, but moving the rail up or down as the bolts are tightened can make slight adjustments.

After the rail bolts are tightened, install the metal or plastic trim (Figure 20-1).

T-RAILS

Although T-rail tables are generally associated with antique tables, many styles and variations of are still being manufactured. Some have exposed leather pockets, some have pocket tops attached to gully return boots for ball returns, and some have metal pocket shields to hide the pockets. Others have aprons or rosettes that cover the rail bolts. Be assured, though, that most of the variations are cosmetic and, therefore, all can be assembled from the following instructions.

Often T-rails can be interchanged as described in Chapter 7, but their bolt holes will not always align properly if they are not returned to their original position.

Leather pockets are usually nailed to the slate tacking board or frame with 1-inch nails before T-rails are installed (see Chapter 21.

To begin the installation of T-rails, set the #2 (side) rail in place and start the rail bolts—but do not tighten. Slide the lug of the center pocket into the hole in that end of the rail (or over the top of the rail if it is a #3 pocket iron) and start the long (usually 4-inch) pocket bolt up through the bottom of the rail base. Again, do not tighten (Figure 20-2).

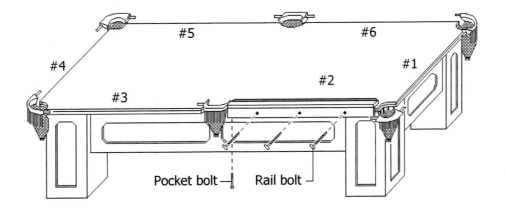

Figure 20-2 *Start with the #2 rail*

Next, position the #3 rail to the left of the same center pocket and start the rail bolts, then the pocket bolt. Insert the corner pocket lug into the end of the #3 rail and start the pocket bolt in that pocket. Continue around the table installing the #4 (foot), #5, and #6 rails and their pockets in like manner.

Trick of the Trade

Older T-rail bolts have a non-standard 16 per inch thread. If bolts are missing or broken, it is often easier to retap the lugs to accept a standard 18 per inch thread, allowing the use of standard hex-head bolts.

The #1 (head) rail and its respective corner pockets should be installed at the same time (Figure 20-3).

Hold the rail at that end of the table, insert a corner pocket lug into each end of the rail, then roll all three (#1 rail and two corner pockets) up together until the two remaining pocket lugs are inserted into rails #2 and #6 simultaneously. Start the bolts in the #1 rail and its two corner pockets. Now, tighten all *rail* bolts.

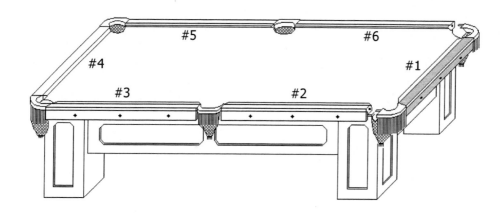

Figure 20-3 *Finish with # 1 rail*

T-rail bolts can be hex-head with standard threads. However, some are nonstandard, thrust-head styles, with two holes that accept a two-prong type tool instead of a standard wrench or socket

(Figure 20-4). Tightening these bolts is a shaky matter because the tool is can pop loose, leaving streaks and gouges in the wood around the bolt heads. Use care.

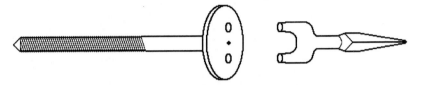

Figure 20-4 *Thrust-head bolt and tool*

Align rails

Next, check to insure that all pockets align with their respective pocket cutouts by looking down into each pocket. T-rails are generally self-aligning because they are bolted to the side of the slate, which keeps them aligned and square (assuming the slate was installed aligned and square, of course).

Use a carpenter's framing square to square the corners, and the straight edge of a carpenter's level to align the side rails with each other (Figure 20-5).

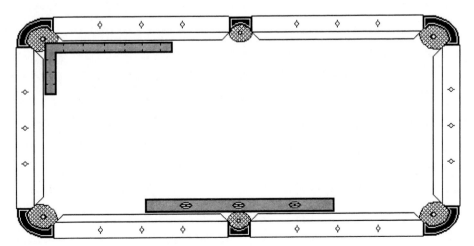

Figure 20-5 *Square and align rails*

If some alignment is needed, small shims between the rail's base and the slate's edge can be used (Figure 20-6).

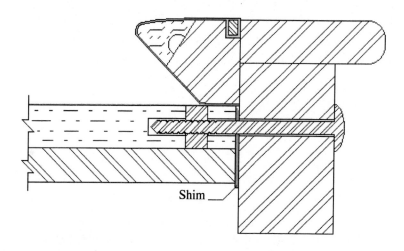

Figure 20-6 *Shim to align, if needed*

After the rails have been squared, aligned, and straightened, tighten all rail and pocket bolts.

Aprons

Finally, install the aprons. They could be individually attached aprons (rail 1 in Figure 20-7), or metal pocket shields and aprons (rail 3 in Figure 20-7). Or they could simply be rosettes (rail 2 in Figure 20-7). The two end aprons are normally an inch or two longer than the four side aprons, and are interchangeable. The four side aprons are often interchangeable on a cater corner basis only.

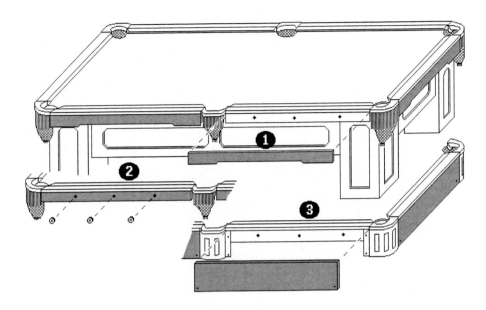

Figure 20-7 *Install rosettes or aprons*

Often, T-rail aprons are attached by the pocket bolts, through the bottom of the apron, and up into the pocket lug. If this is the case, simply back out the pocket bolts, set the aprons in place, and reinsert the pocket bolts.

To secure the pockets, hold each tightly against the rail ends to eliminate gaps, and tighten the pocket bolts. As the bolts are tightened, the back of the pocket may raise 0 to 5 degrees higher than the front to insure that the pocket iron forces the ball down into the pocket (Figure 20-8).

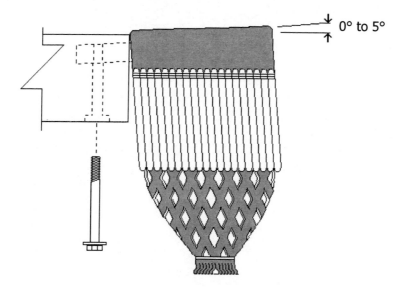

0° to 5°

Figure 20-8 *T-rail pocket*

FLAT RAILS

There are three basic types of flat rail assemblies—leather pocket, mitered or squared with castings, and uniconstructed—and each is assembled somewhat differently.

Flat Rails With Leather Pockets

Be aware that end rails and side rails are different in the way the pocket angles are cut. Therefore, the two end rails are generally interchangeable with each other, but they cannot replace a side rail. Side rails are interchangeable on a cater corner basis only (see Chapter 7).

Attach Pockets to Rails

Pockets are attached to the rails by pocket lugs that are inserted into the holes in the end of the rails. Pocket lugs are drilled and tapped, and are attached to the rail by bolts that penetrate the rail from the bottom (Figure 20-9).

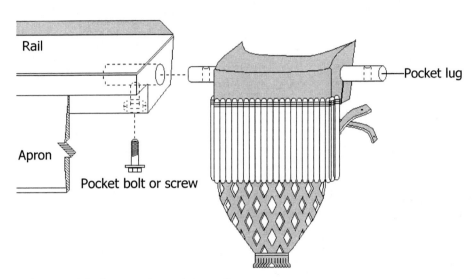

Figure 20-9 *Number 6 iron lugs*

Flat rails with leather pockets are adjustable and must be aligned and squared on the table as they are being installed. These rails will look like T-rails after their installation. Unlike the T-rail, though, leather pockets are assembled onto the rails before they are attached to the table. This can be done by working from under the table with the rails in their usual upright position, but hanging over the edge of the table so the pocket bolts can be reached.

However, assembling the rails and pockets upside-down on the table is much easier. This is done by constructing two horseshoe assemblies (Figure 20-10).

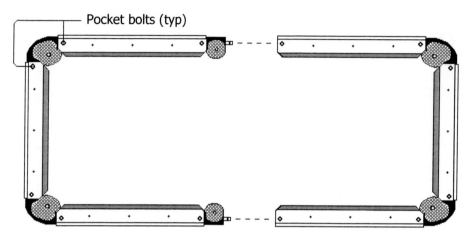

Pocket bolts (typ)

Figure 20-10 *Assemble flat rails upside down*

One assembly consists of an end rail, two side rails, and two corner pockets. The other is the same except that the two center pockets are added to the side rails. Make sure the pockets are snug against the rail ends before the pockets bolts are tightened. If a space is left between a pocket and top rail, the assembly will be weak, and the gap will look unfinished once the table is completed. As the bolts are tightened, the back of the pocket may raise 0 to 5 degrees higher than the front to insure that the pocket iron forces the ball down into the pocket (Figure 20-11).

Caution

Turning each assembly right-side up can be awkward, and could put undue stress on the pocket irons and rails if care is not taken. However, two people can turn the assembly with ease.

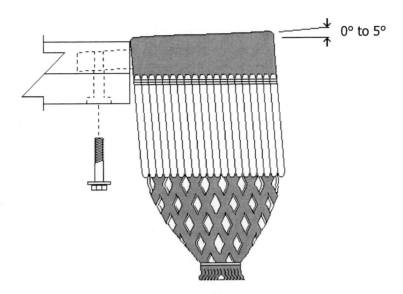

Figure 20-11 *Flat rail pocket*

Pockets with shields (instead of fringe) often come with Velcro tabs to help keep the shield straight and flat. Simply attach the Velcro to the backside of the apron then attach the tabs to the Velcro (Figure 20-12).

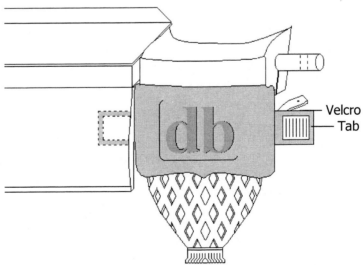

Figure 20-12 *Pockets with shields and tabs.*

Aprons

All flat rail tables have aprons.

Some are often made as a permanent part of the rail (Figure 20-13).

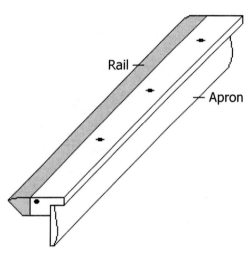

Figure 20-13 *Apron permanently attached to the rail.*

Some are attached before the rails are assembled. The flat bracket style of attachment, for instance, must be fastened to the rails while they are still upside down (Figure 20-14).

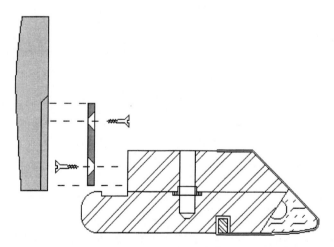

Figure 20-14 *Install flat-bracket aprons before attaching rails.*

The two end aprons are normally an inch or two longer than the four side aprons, and are interchangeable. The four side aprons are often interchangeable on a cater corner basis only.

All the other aprons are installed after the rails are bolted down and usually after the pocket webbing has been affixed to the slate board. Attach them with the provided angle brackets, wood blocks, exposed screws that pass through the face, or some combination (Figure 20-15).

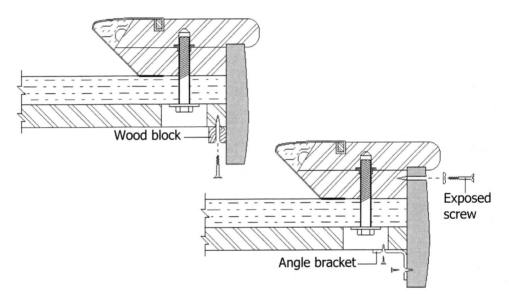

Figure 20-15 *Install these aprons after attaching rails.*

Assemble Rails

The two assemblies are then turned over and positioned on the table. Turning each assembly right-side up can be awkward, and could put undue stress on the pocket irons and rails if care is not taken. However, two people can turn the assembly with ease.

Once the two assemblies have been righted, insert the remaining two center pocket lugs into their respective side rails and screw in the last two pocket bolts from beneath.

Now, start all rail bolts, but do not tighten, the rail must be aligned and squared first (Figure 20-16).

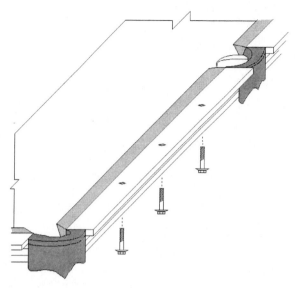

Figure 20-16 *Start all rail bolts*

Caution

Do not bolt all six rails and pockets together and try to turn the whole unit over as one assembly. The points of connection between the center pockets and rails are far too weak for such a maneuver. Also, for the same reason, do not transport the rails in this configuration. A few minutes in tear down time can save many dollars in repair cost.

Next, check to insure that all pockets align with their respective pocket cutouts by looking down into each pocket. The rail assembly can be repositioned and aligned as much as needed before the rail bolts are tightened.

Use a carpenter's framing square to square the corners, and the straight edge of a carpenter's level to align the side rails with each other (Figure 20-17).

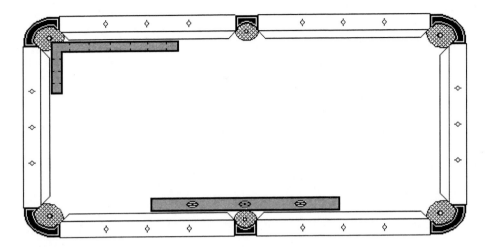

Figure 20-17 *Square and align rails*

After the rails have been squared, aligned, and straightened, tighten all rail bolts, and if needed, attach aprons as shown on page 243.

Next, fasten the pocket webbing to the bottom of the slate tacking board or frame (see Chapter 21)

Mitered or Squared Flat Rails

Mitered or squared flat rails are usually 6 to 8 inches wide and are assembled with corner castings to allow the pockets, or pocket liners if the table has a gully system, to be attached inside the rail assembly. Mitered rails are typically covered with a plastic or metal trim. Squared rails are joined (and trimmed) with metal castings (Figure 20-18).

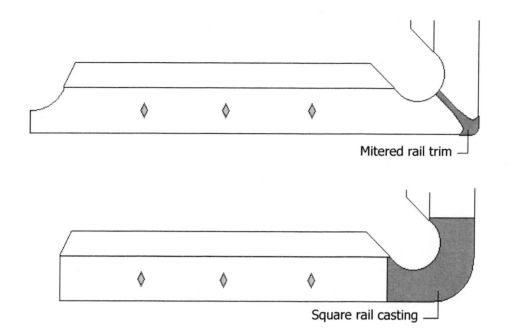

Figure 20-18 *Mitered and squared rails*

Both mitered and squared rails have aprons joined at the corner of the table with plastic or metal corners or castings (Figure 20-19).

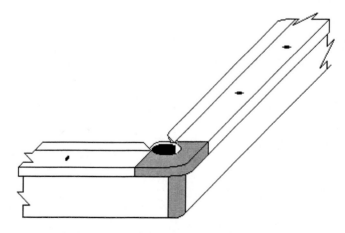

Figure 20-19 *Apron corner casting or trim*

Most of these units, including the aprons and all corner brackets, caps, castings, and cover trims can be assembled right side up with the rails overhanging the table slightly. However, they are usually easier to assemble upside down (Figure 20-20) then, as complete units, carefully rolled over onto their tables.

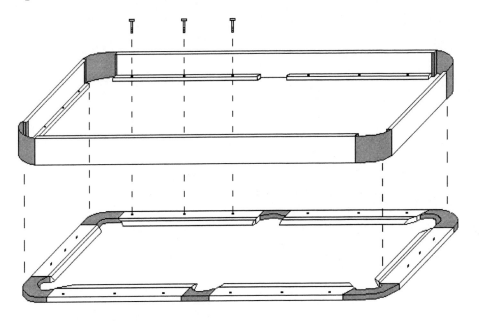

Figure 20-20 *Unit is assembled upside down*

Gully systems that are to be assembled onto the frame should be attached before the rails are installed (see Chapter 21).

Align and Attach Rails

After the rail assembly has been righted, start all rail bolts, but do not tighten. The rails must be aligned and squared before they are

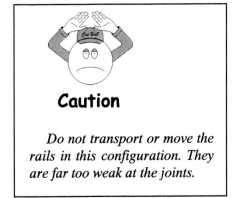

Caution

Do not transport or move the rails in this configuration. They are far too weak at the joints.

secured to the table (Figure 20-21). The best tools for this job are a carpenter's framing square (to square the corners), and the straight edge of a carpenter's level (to align the side rails with each other).

To square and align some square rails, a corner or center rail casting may have to be loosened first then retightened after aligning.

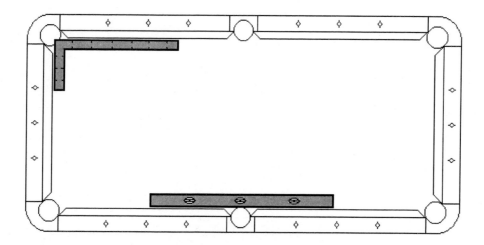

Figure 20-21 *Square and align rails*

Check to insure that all rail pocket cutouts align with their respective slate pocket cutouts by looking down into each pocket hole. The rail assembly can be repositioned as much as needed before the rail bolts are tightened.

After the rails have been aligned, tighten all rail bolts.

Any castings that are misaligned or not flush with the top rail should be readjusted at this time.

Unirails

The unirail system is one in which all six rails are constructed as one unit (Figure 20-22). Simply lay the unit into position on the table, start all rail bolts, then align pocket holes to insure that all rail pocket cutouts align with respective slate pocket cutouts by looking down into each pocket hole. The rail assembly can be repositioned as much as needed before the rail bolts are tightened.

Tighten all rail bolts.

Uniails should not need further adjustments. However, if they are not aligned, the sides can be forced in or out slightly to help align them, but only slightly and with care.

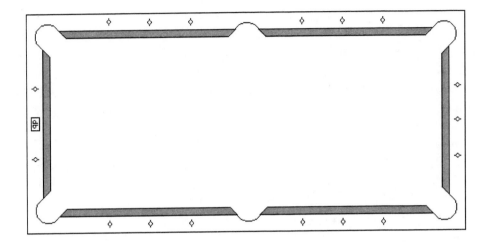

Figure 20-22 *Unirail assemble*

Unirail tables often have a built-in ball return system that uses gullies, with pocket liners instead of pockets. Gully systems that are to be assembled onto the frame should be attached before the rails are installed (see Chapter 21).

Aprons for unirails are usually part of the frame and are installed as the frame is assembled. Otherwise, they will be attached to the rails much like those of a mitered rail assembly.

Trick of the Trade

Often, reaching through or around a gully system to start the rail bolts is impossible. They can, however, be started by using a shallow-well socket and socket extension, which will pass through the ball return gullies with ease.

Words of Experience

A few months ago, I got a phone call from a guy who insisted that he "stole" a pool table for six hundred bucks at a garage sale because the owner was moving. He said it was a massive antique, solid oak table, and he wanted me to move it for him.

The table was massive looking all right, but it was just a standard 8-foot, one-piece slate table with leather pockets. It was not an antique, nor was it solid oak.

On top of the moving charge, the table needed new cushions, new cloth, and new pockets. His steal became a huge dark-brown pink elephant. He had more money in a used table than it was selling for new.

Beware and be aware.

POCKETS

LEATHER POCKETS

With rare exception, tables with T-rails have leather pockets. It is far easier to attach the pockets to the slate tacking board before the rails are installed. This can be done before the bed cloth is installed or after. The only reason to choose one over the other is appearance; covering the leather tabs with the cloth might look better than leaving them exposed. On tables with flat rails, leather pockets should be attached to the rails first then to the slate tacking board after the rails have been installed, as shown in Chapter 20).

Pocket webbing can be attached with $^3/_8$- or $^1/_2$-inch staples, or $^3/_4$-inch nails or screws.

Some new style pockets are made with the tabs connected to each other (Figure 21-1). This can make screwing them to the bottom of the slate tacking board of flat rail tables easier, but usually they must be separated so they can be evenly spaced around the pocket cutout, especially on T-rail tables.

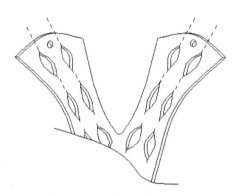

Figure 21-1 *Separate tabs connected to each other, if needed*

T-Rail Tables
        The length of the webbing nailing tabs must be trimmed to fit. Hold each pocket into a pocket cutout approximately where it is to be installed, the top of the pocket will be about $1\frac{1}{2}$ inches above the slate. Holding the rail in position to judge the pocket height may be easier than guessing. Mark the middle four or six tabs at the point where the slate meets the tacking board then cut them so their length of the tabs where they are marked (pocket 1 in Figure 21-2). Most pockets will have six or eight tabs, so the two outside tabs (one on each side) should not be cut or attached to the cutout; they remain outside the cutout and are later nailed to the end of the rail.

Space the nailing tabs equally around the pocket cutout and nail them to the slate tacking board using one-inch nails (pocket 2 in Figure 21-2).

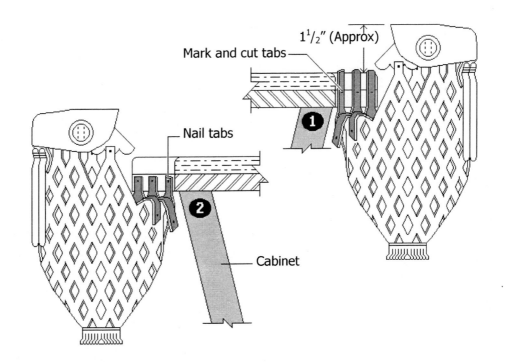

Figure 21-2 *Cut, then nail 4 or 6 tabs to pocket cutout*

Flat Rail Tables

When installing leather pockets on tables with flat rails, the length of the nailing tabs usually do not need to be cut. Instead, they pull under the slate tacking board and are screwed, nailed, or stapled there, beneath the table (Figure 21-3). However, if the tabs are connected to each other (see Figure 21-1) and the leather bunches up then the tabs must be separated. Attach the middle four or six tabs beneath the table. Most pockets will have six or eight tabs, so the two outside tabs (one on each side) should not be attached to the slate board; they are usually nailed to the end of the rail.

Also, if the frame is so close to the pocket cutout that the tabs severely stretch the webbing sideways, then they should be installed to the edge of the pocket cutouts, as if the rails were T-rails (see Figure 21-2).

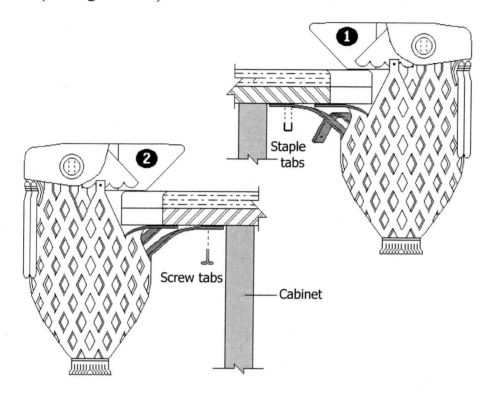

Staple tabs

Screw tabs

Cabinet

Figure 21-3 *Nail, staple, or screw webbing to the slate board*

Both T-Rail and Flat Rail Tables

Inside each leather pocket, between the top leather and the webbing, is a trim sheathing that hides the connection between the webbing and the top leather. To secure that sheathing, each end is usually folded or cut at the edge of the pocket and nailed to the end of the rail (Figure 21-4). The two outside webbing tabs should be nailed onto the rails first, behind the trim sheathing.

Instead of cutting, the excess sheathing is often tucked beneath the rail before the rail is tightened. This is quick and easy, and looks good, but depending on the table, it could raise the cushion nose too high at the end of each rail. Use some restraint.

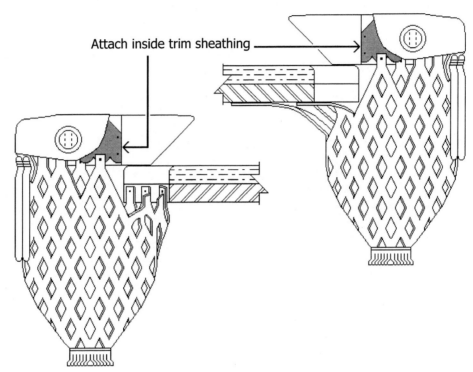

Attach inside trim sheathing

Figure 21-4 *Nail pocket trim*

MOLDED POCKETS
AND POCKET LINERS

Molded pockets or liners can be plastic, rubber, or leather, and are inserted into the pocket cutout from beneath the table; pocket liners are inserted from above, after the rails are installed.

Some tables have smaller pocket cutouts than standard. In these cases, all molded pockets or liners must be trimmed to fit.

Usually, though, only the center pocket or liner needs to be trimmed.

To trim, center the pocket or liner within the cutout. Using a scribe (or a nail), scratch a line from the top edge of the pocket flange, where the rail cloth meets the top rail, down to the top of the pocket basket or bottom of the liner (Figure 21-5).

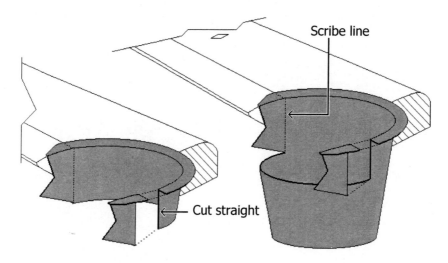

Figure 21-5 *Cut on scribed line*

Remove the pocket or liner and cut along the scribed line. Matching the contour of the rail and slate to make a cut that looks like a > or J is not necessary. A straight vertical cut will look and function fine.

After cutting, reinsert the pocket or liner into position and nail it to the rail. Two 1-inch nails placed slightly behind the rail facing will be sufficient (Figure 21-6), although one at the back of the pocket can be used to keep the pocket solid. The nails do not need to be any larger than 1 inch unless the wood in that area has been chewed up by several previous installations. Some commercial tables with metal pocket castings have provided screws to attach their molded pockets and should be used if possible, but even these pockets can be nailed, if necessary.

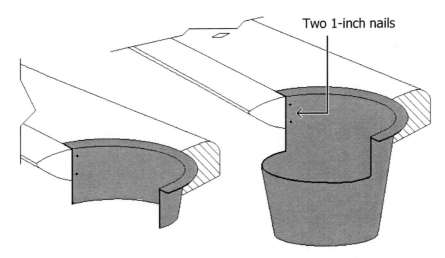

Figure 21-6 *Nail pockets or liners onto rail*

The pocket liners of most coin-operated tables are nailed into the metal castings with spiral nails. Usually the center pocket has no casting, so the liner is simply nailed into the rail like the one shown in Figure 21-6, but not always.

Removing the nails from casting to replace the liners is often tricky to troublesome because the nails usually break before they pull out. If they break, they can usually be drilled with an eighth inch bit, and then replaced.

If that fails, they can be drilled out with a quarter inch bit and replaced with larger plastic pocket nails made for that purpose (Figure 21-7). These nails can be purchased from most billiard suppliers.

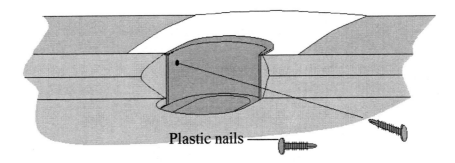

Figure 21-7 *Nail coin-op liners onto castings*

GULLY SYSTEMS

Generally, there are three kinds of gully systems:

1. Those that are built-in and need not be removed or installed.

2. Plastic tubes that connect to plastic gully pockets.

3. Heavy gauge wire tracks that are covered with a plastic coating.

Built in Gullies

Built in gully systems, most often found in coin-operated or home-style tables, have tracks made of fiberglass, plastic, wood, or sometimes, even cardboard. These systems also have a gully boot to direct the ball to the track. Gully boots and pocket liners are often molded, sewn, or riveted together, but usually they are separate pieces (Figure 21-8).

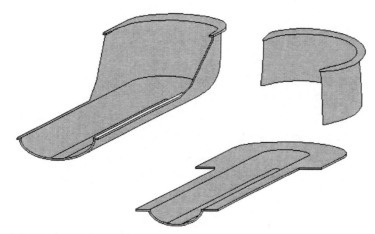

Figure 21-8 *Attach gully boot to frame*

Most gully boots are manufactured with flanges along the back and side for attaching to the frame cutouts. Gully boot attachment can be made using nails, screws, or staples. Occasionally, though, pool table manufacturers remove the flanges (or use boots made without flanges) and attach the boot through the sidewalls. Often some are attached with a single screw through the end at the bottom of the gully (Figure 21-9).

To insure correct installation of the new boot, the old boot must be removed carefully. Each screw, nail, or staple should be removed without splitting or splintering the frame member. The old boot can be used as a template for sizing the new one.

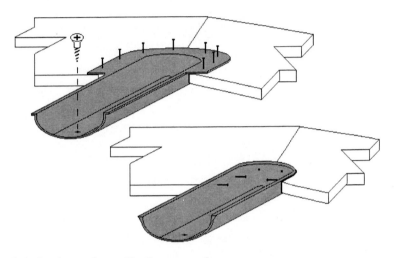

Figure 21-9 *Attach gully boot to frame*

The boots on most coin-operated tables are simply screwed onto the ball track with one screw (Figure 21-10). The slate must be removed.

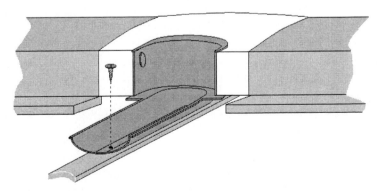

Figure 21-10 *Attach coin-op boot to ball track*

Plastic Tubing Gullies

A set of plastic tubing gullies consists of six gully pockets and four tubes. The tubes are all the same diameter and length, but there are three different heights of gully pockets: two short, two medium, and two tall (Figure 21-11).

All short gully pockets have one connecting hole for gully tubes. These pockets are installed at the head of the table with the gully hole pointing toward the foot. Medium pockets have two opposing gully holes, one smaller than the other. The smaller hole points toward the foot of the table. The tallest pockets also have two gully holes, but they are at right angles to each other. The smaller of these two holes point into the ball box.

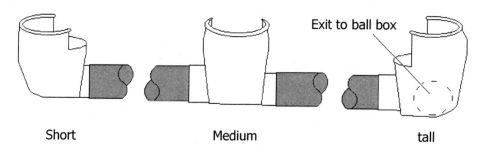

Short   Medium   tall

Figure 21-11 *Plastic tube gully system*

Plastic gully pockets are installed after the rails have been attached to the table. They are installed just as if they were any other molded pockets except that the gully tubes must be inserted into the connecting pocket holes before the pockets are nailed into place.

The gully tubes fit *over* the connecting holes of the pockets at the high end, and *into* the connecting holes of the pockets at the low end. This allows for a smooth ball transfer when it rolls through the system (Figure 21-11)

Wire Gully Systems

Most wire gully systems have four separate tracks: two head and two foot. The head tracks are straight, and the foot tracks have a 90-degree bend at one end. This bend allows the balls to turn into a ball collection box.

Four or five attaching brackets extend up from each track. The longest brackets are at the ball box end of the table, and the shortest are at the head. If the tops of these brackets are pushed up against the slate tacking board or table frame and attached to the base frame there, the track will, by design, pitch from the head to the foot of the table (Figure 21-12).

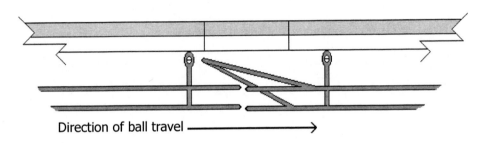

Direction of ball travel ⟶

Figure 21-12 *Wire gully system*

Wire gully systems are installed before the rails are attached to the table.

Install the foot tracks first by setting the short bent end in the ball box, pushing the hanging brackets into place and screwing them to the base frame. Then, at the center, align the head tracks with the foot tracks, and attach them to the base frame. At the point of connection, the head tracks can be slightly higher than the foot tracks but not lower. The ball must transfer smoothly between the tracks (Figure 21-12).

Ball Collection Box

All gully systems have a box that collects the balls from the gully returns. Ball boxes either hang on the bottom of the frame or are built into the table. Ball boxes that hang onto the frames are installed when the frames are set up (Figure 21-13), and those built into the table are either installed when the aprons are assembled, or are preinstalled.

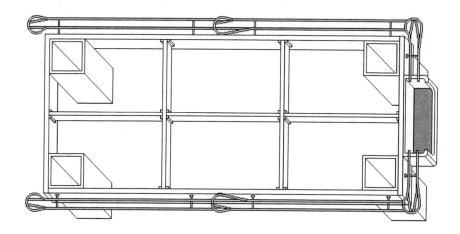

Figure 21-13 *Ball collection box*

Coin-operated and other one-piece slate tables have built-in ball boxes and gully systems, and never need to be removed (Figure 21-14).

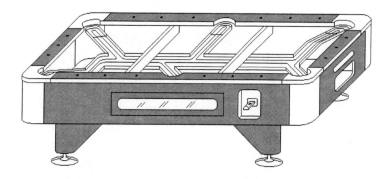

Figure 21-14 *Coin-operated table*

VI
Repairs

The life and beauty of a pool table and its accessories can be preserved for years by performing routine maintenance. Pool table maintenance is often overlooked because it is forgotten, or perceived as difficult or unimportant. In reality, it can be quite easy, and extremely important.

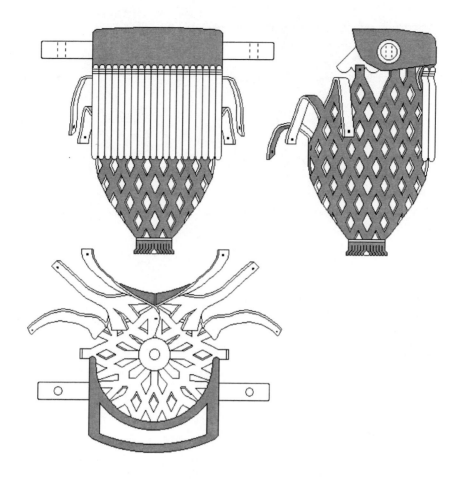

IN THIS SECTION

Chapter 22. Repairs

REPAIRS

The most important act an owner can do to preserve a pool table and its accessories is to maintain them properly. That is basic advice. It does not matter what kind of equipment it is, it needs to be maintained before it will produce a respectable amount of serviceability.

BILLIARD CLOTH

A simple matter of brushing the billiard cloth after each session of play will prolong its life immeasurably, and a quality (horsehair bristle) table brush should be used. Synthetic bristle brushes are better than nothing, but they are stiff and sharp and pull the cloth nap, creating a disturbing amount of fuzz (pills) that could shorten the life of the cloth.

It is important that the table be brushed in straight, overlapping strokes toward the foot end of the table. This brushing method is taken from directional cloth because of its need to be brushed with the lay of the nap. However, even non-directional cloth nap will lean in the direction it is brushed. If the cloth is brushed in arcs, the travel of a slow-moving ball can be influenced by the brush marks, making the table appear off level. This effect is usually called cloth or nap roll, and it is imperative that the roll is in a straight line, preferably head to foot.

A small or weak vacuum cleaner is okay to use when cleaning chalk, dust, and such from the cloth, providing the attachment head is a soft non-rotating brush. Rotating brushes and beater bars cause unneeded wear on the cloth. Lint and pet hair can be easily removed with a lint roller or masking tape.

Trick of the Trade

A little water will shrink the cloth, causing it to tighten. In some cases, this can save the trouble of dismantling the rails to re-stretch a loose bed cloth.

Cloth can be cleaned with a billiard cloth brush, cool water with mild soap, used sparingly. Generally, because the cloth is made of wool and nylon, water will do it little harm, as long as it's attached to the table, otherwise it'll shrink beyond use. The color may fade a bit but that is about all.

A product like Woolite can also be used to clean soiled spots such as soft drinks and beer spills. Use a terry cloth towel to absorb the spill, and then lightly wash the entire playing surface to prevent a cleaned spot where the soiled area was.

Do not soak the cloth to the point of saturating the playing surface, though. This is especially important on three-piece slate tables or tables made of particle boards. A favorite compound used to fill the joints of three-piece slates is water-soluble putty. Water putty does an excellent job, but if it gets wet, it becomes putty again, which can re-dry in lumps, bumps, or pits. Also, when particle board is soaked it can warp, expand, chip, or crack.

As a preventive measure, a fitted dust cover is an excellent way to protect billiard cloth from direct sunlight, accidental spills, pets, and of course dust.

Repairing Rips

Three repairs can be made to fix small rips in the bed cloth, although not generally used because of the minute, but still undesirable, obstructions left behind. The cloth can be sewn, glued, or patched; each is as good as the others (Figure 22-1).

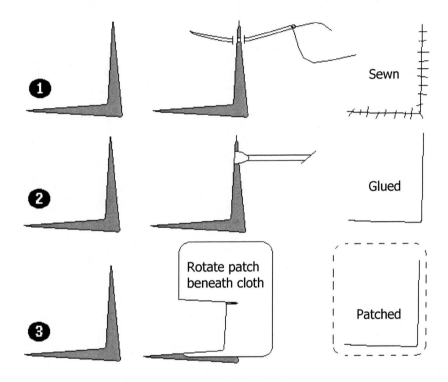

Figure 22-1 *Repair ripped bed cloth*

To sew a rip, use thin nylon thread, preferably the same color as the cloth, and a small curved needle. Both can be purchased from a sewing shop. The stitches should be close enough to each other to pull the rip together, but not so close as to cause unnecessary bulk (repair 1 in Figure 22-1).

To glue a rip, use contact cement and a cotton swab. Apply a small amount of the cement to the backside of the cloth and to the slate around the rip. Allow the cement to dry for a few minutes then pull the rip together and press it to the slate (repair 2 in Figure 22-1).

To patch a rip, use an iron-on patch inserted beneath the cloth (repair 3 in Figure 22-1). Iron-on patches can also be purchased from any sewing shop. The patch should be slightly larger than the rip. A slit half way through the patch will help to rotate it beneath the rip. It can also simply be folded, then unfolded once under the cloth. Use a *dry* iron set at 325 to 350 degrees Fahrenheit. Preheat the area before slipping the patch into place. Do not allow the iron to scorch the billiard cloth; a thin ironing cloth between the iron and billiard cloth may help. Follow any specific instructions that come with the iron-on patch.

BALLS

When balls are new, it is quite simple to keep them clean with vinegar and water, or a window cleaner like Windex. However, all phenolic balls will mar and yellow over time even if they're washed daily. A household cleaning product like Comet or Ajax, or less abrasive Soft Scrub, does a wonderful job if the balls are not too terrible. For extremely yellowed balls, use a paint stripper, like Zip Strip. Read the instructions of the product and wear protective clothing.

Although any of these products may also strip the shine from the balls, good wax will return most of the luster. Liquid wax and furniture wax will work, but paste wax is better.

Some billiard stores and poolrooms have ball cleaning and polishing machines that use a wool buffer, and jeweler's rouge or ball cleaner. These machines usually do an exceptional job and are a lot less messy than hand cleaning.

Cracked or chipped balls should be discarded. They can do more harm to the billiard cloth than the cost of a replacement ball.

CUES

Unless specifically purchased without, most cue shafts come with a urethane or varnish finish. This finish should be removed with extra-fine 600-grit sandpaper or 0000-grit steel wool. Lightly sand about ten inches from the ferrule toward the joint—the distance of a pro-taper. The cue should never be sanded again. Some players have a habit of sanding the shaft occasionally to keep it slick and smooth. Over time, this makes the shaft smaller in diameter. A better method is to use a cloth dampened with a solution of cool water and mild soap. Wipe the mixture on and off quickly. Do not soak. From then on, as sweat and dirt build up, use a small synthetic household scrub pad like Scotch Bright (but not steel wool) to keep the shaft clean and

Trick of the Trade

To clean a shaft, use cool water and mild soap, and a synthetic scrub pad to keep it clean. Talc and powers are not necessary.

slick. Nothing else, not even powder or talc, is needed. Actually, powder and talc are self-defeating, the more they are used the dirtier the shaft becomes. The dirtier the shaft is, the more it will need to be powdered. It is simply not necessary when a damp cloth and scrub pad will do the job better. Also, a few products on the market are designed to make a cue slick without powders, sandpaper, or mess, and are worth trying.

A cue should never be leaned against the pool table or wall, even between shots. If possible, try to stand the cue straight up in a rack. If it must be supported by the table or wall, keep it as perpendicular as possible, with no side load on the shaft. Laying a cue flat on the playing surface is okay for short periods, but avoid storing it like that. When a cue is lying flat, the tip end of the shaft may not be supported, and gravity will eventually take its toll.

Always store one-piece cues in a rack, either floor or wall mounted. Break down two-piece cues and store them in a case, preferably one that is hard and sturdy. Do not store any cue in places of extreme temperature and humidity variances, such as cars, attics, damp basements, etc.

Ferrule Replacement

Ferrules are sleeves or points installed onto the end of the cue shaft to prevent the wood from splitting or splintering.

Ferrules are made of plastic, fiber, Lucite, or phenolic. Plastic ferrules are used on inexpensive cues, and Lucite or phenolic on higher priced custom cues. Fiber ferrules are generally used on one-piece house cues, but can be found on some inexpensive custom cues. The length can vary from 1/2 inch to a little over 1 inch.

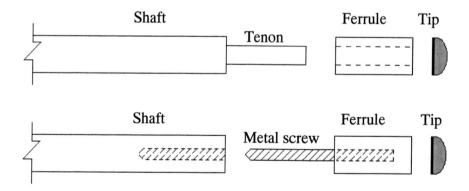

Figure 22-2 *Ferrules*

Ferrules can be installed with wood glue or epoxy onto a tenon cut into the end of the shaft, or screwed onto metal screws that are implanted into the shaft end (Figure 22-2).

The inside diameter of the ferrule should match the diameter of the tenon, and the outside diameter of the ferrule should be the same as the cue shaft and tip. If the diameter of the replacement ferrule is larger than the shaft, it can be filed, sanded, or turned on a lathe to match.

Tip Replacement

Cue tips are merely discs of tanned leather in some variance of compression from soft to hard. Some expensive tips are chemically treated with a finishing polish, compressed and calibrated for hardness. Some are infused with chalk to prevent miscuing, others are simply pressed, stamped leather and are not treated in any fashion. A vinyl or leather base is often bonded to the back of the tip to facilitate adhesion to the ferrule.

Soft tips take chalk better than hard, but hard tips have greater durability. Cuing the ball causes soft tips to compress and conform to the ball's shape, allowing for maximum contact. This makes soft tips more forgiving and less prone to miscuing. Hard tips, on the other hand, will not give or contort when they strike the cue ball. Hard tips must be chalked often, stroked with precision, and the cue ball must be hit closer to center to prevent miscuing.

Replacing a cue tip seems to give people more trouble than any other aspect of pool table and accessory maintenance. In fact, it is such a nuisance that it has led to the miserable slip-on tip. Slip-on tips consist of a tip pre-glued onto a thin-shelled ferrule that slips over the original ferrule, or bare shaft end. They do not last long, look terrible, and play even worse than they look.

The greatest frustration with replacing cue tips is that the glue never holds. This occurs for two reasons. One, the two surfaces are not properly cleaned, and two, the glue used is usually the wrong kind. Instant glues, hot glues, spray glues, and glues that come in tipping kits do not work. What does work? Contact cement and two-part epoxy.

Trick of the Trade

Two-part, five-minute epoxy is an excellent cue tip glue. Two-part epoxy can be purchased from any hardware store.

To replace a tip, use one that is somewhat larger in diameter than that of the ferrule. Sand the base of the tip and the top of the ferrule as flat as possible with rough sandpaper—sanding wheels and machines are okay but not required. Apply a small amount of glue to both the ferrule and tip. Gingerly press the two together, but do not squeeze all of the glue from between them (contact type cement must become tacky or dry before the two are pressed together).

It is not necessary to use a rubber band or clamp to hold the tip in place. Simply hold the cue upright until the glue is sufficiently dried so the tip doesn't slip, then set it aside to allow the glue to cure.

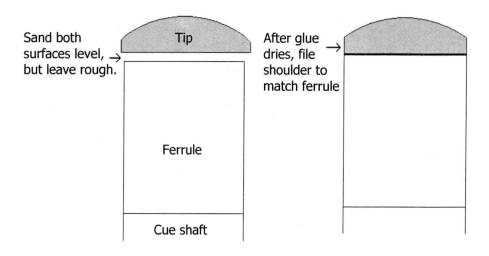

Figure 22-3 *Replacing a cue tip*

After the glue has cured, sand or file the shoulder (edge) of the tip until it is flush with the side of the ferrule. Push the file or sandpaper down toward the ferrule; never drag either up or away from the ferrule. This pulling motion can cause the tip fibers to separate. Also, take care not to sand the ferrule (Figure 22-3).

The cue tip should be rough to hold chalk, and crowned so a rounded surface will be striking the ball. However, a shoulder should be left between the beginning of the crown and the tip's base at the top of the ferrule. This insures a good tip to ball contact. A good rule-of-thumb is that the crown of the tip should have the same arc as the circumference of a U.S. penny, with a shoulder of not less than $^1/_{16}$ inch (Figure 22-4).

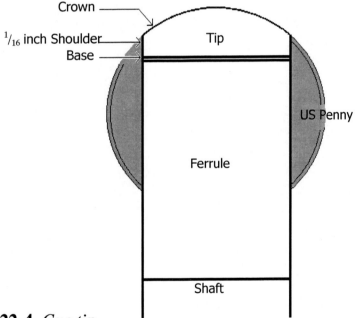

Figure 22-4 *Cue tip*

Instead of a penny, some players use a nickel, while others prefer a dime. The arc of a penny falls between those two, and has an almost ideal circumference. Several cue tip shaping tools now on

Trick of the Trade

If a clamp is used to hold the tip while the glue dries, do not use the slide ring that holds the clamp to the shaft because it will indent or ding the wood. Instead, twist a rubber band over the clamp and shaft. After the glue dries, simply cut the rubber band to remove the clamp.

the market make the job a snap, but the crown can be shaped with a file or 60-grit sandpaper, if care is taken. Again, always sand down toward the ferrule.

Cue tips compress and flatten during play, and should be reshaped periodically.

LEATHER POCKETS

Leather pockets are the most neglected hardware on a pool or snooker table. They are subject to drying, cracking, and deteriorating like any organic material. The leather of the pockets can be kept soft and pliable for years by simply using a good leather conditioner every six months or so. Apply the conditioner to the inside and the outside of each pocket. If the pockets are excessively dry, give them a second coat after the first has been absorbed.

After the conditioning, leather pockets can be cleaned and polished with shoe dye and shoe polish.

Mending Leather Pockets

Small rips in the leather webbing can be mended using leather lace, wire, electrical wiring ties, or nylon strings the same color as the webbing (Figure 22-5).

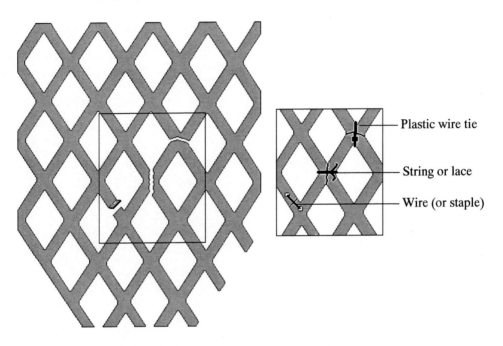

Plastic wire tie

String or lace

Wire (or staple)

Figure 22-5 *Repair leather webbing*

If the rip is between webbing cutouts, wrap the mending material through the webbing, around the rip, pull snug, and tie. If the rip is across a piece of webbing, punch holes through the leather, one on each side of the rip, then thread the mending material through the holes and tie. A $^1/_2$-inch staple also works, simply drive it across the rip, and bend the legs on the other side.

Place the knots outside the webbing where they will be hidden by the pocket fringe and table frame. The repair should hold as well as the original webbing if the knot is secure.

Leather pockets can also be repaired by replacing badly torn webbing with plastic pockets (Figure 22-6). To make the repair, cut the old webbing from the top leather, but do not remove the stitching or rivets that hold the top leather onto the pocket iron (rail 1 in Figure 22-6).

Next, trim and insert the plastic pocket into the pocket hole as if it were being installed on a table with mitered rails (see Chapters 20 and 21). Nail the plastic pocket to the end of each rail.

The pocket iron and top leather are used as a back or frame for the plastic pocket, and the decorative fringe will hide most of the plastic from direct view (rail 2 in Figure 22-6).

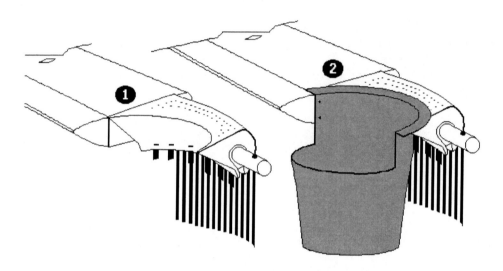

Figure 22-6 *Replace webbing with plastic*

This may not be the best repair, but it is inexpensive, functional, and the pockets do not have to be removed from the table to make the repair.

Broken pocket irons usually cannot be mended, and should be replaced when possible to save wear on the top leather and balls. Each leather pocket consists of five components: top leather, iron, webbing, inside trim sheathing, and fringe (Figure 22-7).

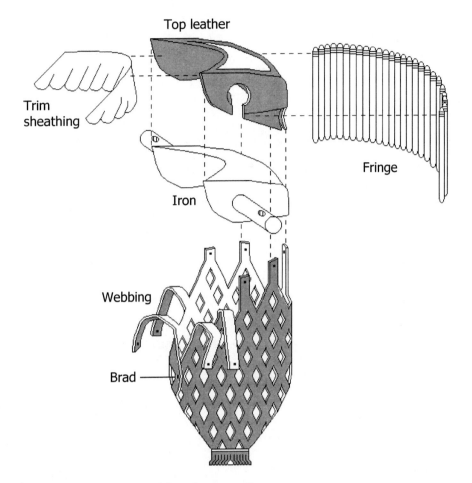

Figure 22-7 *Typical leather pocket*

To replace any of the pocket components, remove the pocket from the table, and cut the stitching (or rivets) that holds the top leather to the irons. Care must be taken not to cut any reusable piece.

The top leather is pre-formed to fit the iron size and shape, and is simply slipped from the iron.

To reassemble, slip the top leather onto the iron, evenly insert the five or six large webbing tabs between the top leather halves, and rivet or sew them into place. The tabs are opposite the brad that holds the webbing together, and usually have pre-punched rivet holes.

All sewing must be done with a heavy-duty leather machine, such as that used by a leather shop or shoe shop. Rivets can be expanding rivets, pop rivets, or split rivets

The inside trim sheathing and fringe can be sewn or glued onto the pocket.

Gluing is accomplished by using contact cement. Brush cement onto both the outside and inside of the pocket and the backside of the trim sheathing and fringe, allow it to become tacky, then press the pieces together.

All pocket parts are available from most pool table supply companies.

Replacing any of these parts, however, is not an easy task, nor is it necessarily cheap. Often, purchasing a new set of pockets is simply better.

Trick of the Trade

If rivets are not available, small machine screws, washers, and lock nuts can be used. The nuts should be placed outside the pocket.

Antique Pockets

When antique tables are being restored, having the original pocket irons re-leathered to insure proper fit is often imperative. Broken irons can usually be welded before they are re-leathered, and odd $5/16$-16 threaded lugs can be re-tapped to accept a standard $5/16$-18 bolt. Recasting nonstandard irons, although possible, is often cost prohibitive. Also, soaking an ill fitting #6 top leather with linseed oil, or similar fat, then reforming it to fit a #5—or a #3 to fit a #G—is often possible.

All pocket components can be purchased from any pool table supply company.

Knit pockets are usually attached by wire retainers as opposed to the nailing tabs of leather pockets shown in Chapter 8.

By the way, knit pockets are still handmade. So, if grandma can knit . . .

RAILS AND CABINETS

All wood on pool tables should be treated like the wood on any furniture. Regular oiling and waxing are essential in keeping it from drying and cracking.

Small scars, scratches, etc. can be covered with a household scratch-covering product, and there are lots available. I like Old English because it stains, seals, and finishes in one coat.

Laminated tables should also be cleaned and waxed periodically.

Keep all tables from direct sunlight to prevent fading, sun-bleaching, or rapid drying. A dust cover that covers the entire table instead of just the playing surface helps a great deal.

Although not simple or particularly easy, rails damaged along the feather strip can be repaired. These unsightly chips and dings, especially on laminated rails (most often caused by players banging their cues on the rails) can be fixed by widening the feather strip grooves past the chips, then using a wider feather strips (Figure 22-8). A table router with a fence guide is recommended, but a hand-held router with an adjustable guide works if care is taken.

Most feather strips are roughly $^1/_4$ inch wide, but there is no reason they cannot be wider—they will hold just as effectively. Wider feather strips must be specifically made to fit the wider groove, or using two narrow strips instead of one wide strip is often possible.

Follow the instructions in Chapter 17 for feather strip installation.

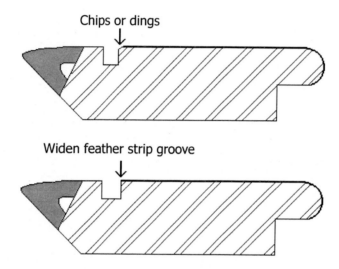

Figure 22-8 *Widen grooves to eliminate chips*

Worn, elongated, or split pocket lug holes can be repaired in a couple of ways, one fairly easy and the other more difficult. The easy way, if the hole is only elongated or isn't otherwise excessively damaged (rail 1 in Figure 22-9), is to use metal inserts or spacers placed beneath the pocket lug, at the bottom of the hole (rail 2 in Figure 22-9). This acts as a shim to help fill the hole and to strengthen the wood. Pocket lug inserts can be made from electrical conduit or purchased from most pool table supply store.

The difficult way, when the wood is broken or pieces are missing from the base rail, around the hole (rail 1 in Figure 22-8), is to replace the damaged wood out. Cut a square roughly 3 inches by 3 inches by the depth of the base rail. I've found that a router with a cutting tip is ideal to remove the old wood. Replace the removed wood with a new piece the same size. Use a drill press to redrill the holes (rail 4 in Figure 22-9).

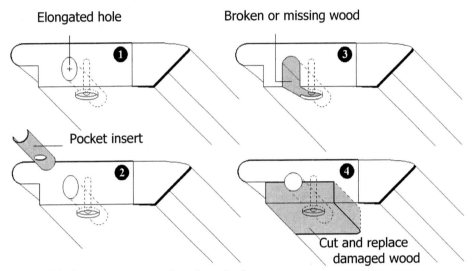

Figure 22-9 *Repair pocket lug holes*

CUSHIONS

Cushion nose height is determined and set during cushion installation. If necessary, cushion height can be slightly changed by shimming the rails during their installation. Shimming between the rail and the slate, behind the rail bolts before they are tightened, can lower cushions that are too high. Conversely, cushions that are too low can be raised slightly by shimming in front of the rail bolts (Figure 22-10). This change should not be more than $^1/_{16}$ inch either way. If more than that is required, it is better to reinstall the cushions to their proper height.

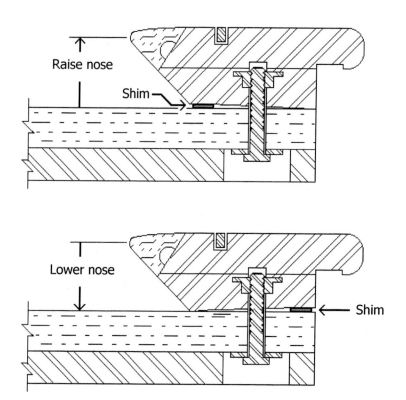

Figure 22-10 *Adjust cushion nose height*

Most non-conforming cushions are glued to a square or straight rail face. Full profile cushions are glued to a rail that has been cut at an angle of about 20° from the square. This angle is approximate and must be calculated to insure that the cushion nose height meets the ball slightly above center (see "Cushion Height" in Chapter 1).

Re-cutting a rail that has non-conforming cushions to accept full profile cushions, without changing the table's playing surface dimensions or the cushion nose height, is possible. This can be accomplished if the rail is solid wood or tightly compressed particle board. Also, the shoulder between the feather strip groove and the finished cut should not be less than $^3/_8$ inch (Figure 22-11), which could weaken the rail significantly.

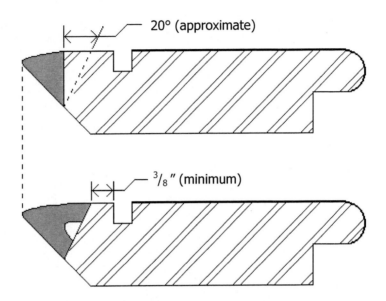

Figure 22-11 *Re-cut rail to accept full profile cushions*

SLATE

Some breaks, chips, and cracks in the slate can often be repaired to make the slate as functional as a new piece (Figure 22-12).

Cracks can be filled with two-part epoxy to prevent the crack from opening further. Use a putty knife to push the epoxy deep into the crack. If the epoxy does not penetrate through the slate, fill the crack on both sides.

Chips and holes can be filled with auto body putty, then smoothed and sanded to match the surface of the slate. Make sure all loose pieces of slate and dust are removed before filling.

Clean breaks can be reinforced with a backing board screwed onto the slate. Use countersunk flathead wood screws, or flathead bolts with washers and lock nuts. Epoxy the pieces of slate together before attaching them to the backing board, then fill the screw holes with auto body putty. See Chapter 15 for a discussion on how to drill holes into slate.

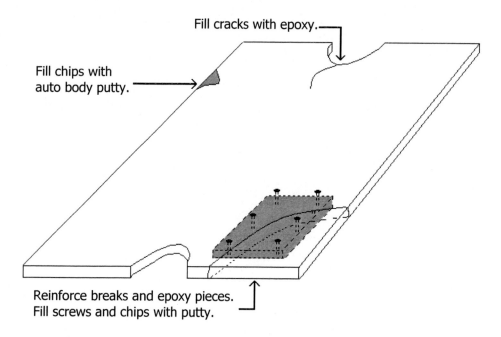

Figure 22-12 *Slate repairs*

COIN-OPERATED TABLES

Coin-chutes

Most modern coin-op table coin-chutes can be set up to accept multiple coins (usually quarters). The process of changing these is simply a matter of removing a plastic plug and replacing it with a metal slot that accepts the coin. Any new coin chute should come with an instruction sheet explaining the process for that particular chute. Figure 22-13 shows how a common chute can be changed over to accept more coins.

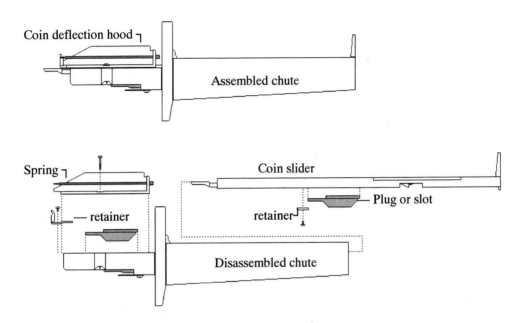

Figure 22-13 *Coin-chute*

The chute must be removed from the table door and all accessories, like striker bars and counters, detached from the chute. Release the two springs on the deflection hood, then remove the deflection hood. There is a storage area for extra plugs and slots beneath the hood.

Extract the screw that holds the spring retainer, which also holds the plugs and slots in the storage area.

Next, pull the coin slider out. Beneath the coin slider, extract the two or three screws from the retainer that hold the plugs and slots in place.

Exchange the plug or slot according to your needs and replace the retainer. Replace the coin slider. If it jams, simply tilt the whole mechanism to the left. This allows the coin stops in the housing to fall clear so the coin slider can slip into place.

Return any extra plugs or slots to the storage area and replace the spring retainer.

Replace the deflection hood and reattach the two springs.

Put all the accessories back and reinstall the chute.

Cue ball returns

There are four mechanisms or methods that force the cue ball to the break end of the table.

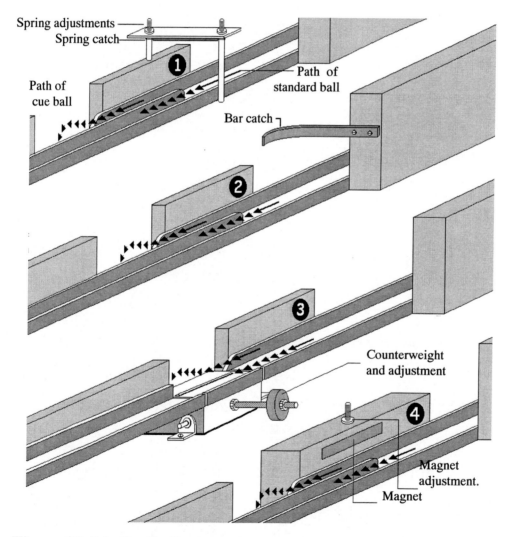

Figure 22-14 *Cue ball returns*

The first is simply a spring that catches an oversize cue ball forcing it to the side while allowing a standard ball to pass beneath it (track 1 in Figure 22-14). There is a small amount of adjustment in raising or lowering one end or the other of the spring.

Next, is a bar that also catches an oversize cue ball sending it to the side while allowing a standard ball to pass beneath it (track 2 in Figure 22-14). Some bars have adjustment screws and others can be bent slightly up or down for adjustment.

The third mechanism is a counterweighted pivot, which is used to trip when the oversize (and overweight) cue ball passes over it, but does not trip with a standard size (and weight) ball (track 3 in Figure 22-14). The counterweight on the pivot can be turned in or out for adjustment.

The most prominent and effective mechanism is a magnet that traps an iron impregnated or iron core cue ball sending it to the side while allowing a standard ball to pass (track 4 in Figure 22-14). Some tables have adjusting nuts for the magnets, but most don't.

Of course, some tables are set up to use two methods at the same time. This is done to insure that the system works smoothly or so that either an oversize or a standard size cue balls can be used. The combination usually found is the magnet and bar catch, or the magnet and counterweight.

Usually there's a fine balance between a method that works and one that doesn't. So tinkering is the norm to get the adjustments right. Have fun.

Clean-outs

To prevent the tracks from becoming blocked with small items like chalk, small slots are provided in the tracks or boots. But most coin-operated tables have two or more gully cleanouts for larger items like toys, tennis balls, ashtrays, etc. that can and will block the system.

Some tables have a trap door at the bottom and some do not. Most have a small clean-out door at the break end of the table, which allows access to the main track. And, last but not least, it is often possible to remove the side door to reach blocks.

LEVELING

Usually, when a table is installed on a hard floor and leveled properly at the time of installation, it will not need to be re-leveled. That is, however, rarely the case because more tables are being installed on carpet these days than ever. Carpet is okay, but the table must be re-leveled until it settles to the point of crushing the carpet padding, then it should remain level. If the carpet is thin, with little or no padding, the table will settle quickly and may not need to be re-leveled.

Also, a pool table can weigh from four hundred pounds to as much as a ton. Houses or rooms with floor joist systems (beams that supports floors with rooms, basements, or crawl spaces beneath them) will settle with the addition of the pool table's weight. As this occurs, the table will need re-leveling.

To help maintain the table's levelness, remember these three old rules:

1. Never, sit on the table.
2. Always, have one foot on the floor when shooting.
3. Never, pick up a table to move it, or to dislodge a ball.

In the event a table needs to be re-leveled, follow the procedures described in the installation section of this book, especially "Fine Tuning the Levelness" in Chapter 15.

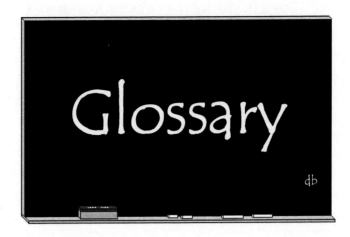

APRONS: A decorative board connected to the side of a rail to hide the edge of the slate, tacking board, and parts of the frame. Aprons are also called blinds, fascia boards, and shields.

BACKED SLATE: Backing boards are attached to the bottom of some slate to help preserve the slate's flatness. The boards are also used to staple the bed cloth to the table.

BACKED CLOTH: Some billiard cloth has vinyl adhered to the back or underside to make the cloth rip resistant.

BALLS: Originally, pool balls were made of wood, then clay (mud balls), then ivory, and now phenolic. Because they stay round, are consistent in weight, and are less likely to crack or chip, phenolic balls are far superior to any of the others.

 A standard phenolic resin pool ball weighs 6 ounces and has a diameter of $2^1/_4$ inches. A traditional set of balls consists of fifteen numbered balls and one cue ball. The cue ball is white, the first eight numbered balls are a solid color, and the remaining seven have colored stripes. The typical color scheme shown below.

Ball color	Solid number	Striped number
White	Cue ball	- -
Yellow	1 ball	9 ball
Blue	2 ball	10 ball
Red	3 ball	11 ball
Purple	4 ball	12 ball
Orange	5 ball	13 ball
Green	6 ball	14 ball
Burgundy	7 ball	15 ball
Black	8 ball	- -

Common carom balls weigh $7^1/_4$ ounces each with a diameter of $2^3/_8$ inches. Other acceptable carom balls weigh between 7 and $7^1/_2$-ounces with diameters of $22^7/_{64}$ and $2^7/_{16}$ inches. A standard set of carom balls consists of three balls—two white cue balls and one red object ball. One cue ball has a distinguishing mark, usually a small circle or dot.

Snooker balls weigh $5^1/_4$ to $5^1/_2$ ounces and have a diameter of $2^1/_8$ inches (the most common), or in some cases $2^1/_{16}$ inches. A set of snooker balls consists of fifteen red balls and six colored balls. Each of the six colored balls has a specific value that is usually, but not always, numbered to reflect that value.

Ball color	Ball number
Red	(not numbered)
Black	7 ball
Pink	6 ball
Blue	5 ball
Brown	4 ball
Green	3 ball
Yellow	2 ball

Rebound pool balls should be $2^1/_8$ inches in diameter and weigh approximately $5^1/_4$ ounces. A set of rebound pool balls consists of two groups of five non-numbered balls. One group is usually red, the other white. The break ball of each group is distinguished by a large dot of the opposite color.

BALL BOX: A box that collects the balls from a gully return system.

BCA: Billiard Congress of America. BCA is America's most prominent billiard regulating group.

BED: The part of the table that becomes the playing surface once the table is assembled.

BED CLOTH: The billiard cloth attached to the bed.

BILLIARD CLOTH: A woven fabric made of 100% wool or a blend of 75% wool and 25% nylon or 80% wool and 20% nylon. Typical cloth weights 20 to 22 ounces.

BILLIARD FABRIC: A woven fabric made of wool or a blend of wool and nylon. See Billiard Cloth.

BILLIARDS: All billiard games including Carom, Pool, Snooker, etc.

BRIDGE: 1. A hand bridge is a support made by a player's hand to hold a pool cue level and firm while playing the game.
2. Mechanical bridges are designed for two purposes. One is to allow a player to extend across the table for a shot that could not otherwise be reached. The other is to allow a player to play over a ball that has blocked the cue ball. Mechanical bridges are usually stored on hooks, within easy reach, beneath one side of the table.

BRUSHES: There are two kinds of pool table brushes that should be used on billiard cloth.
      The common bed cloth brush is used to brush the playing surface. Quality bed cloth brushes are approximately ten inches long

and have horsehair bristles. The bristles on the ends are longer than those in the middle so the brush can be used beneath the cushion overhang.

The other brush is strictly for cleaning beneath the cushion overhang. This brush is handy but not essential. Because of its plastic bristles, it should be used sparingly, lightly, and only beneath the cushion overhang.

CABINET: The exposed portion of any table.

CAROM: 1. Carom is the deflection of one ball from another ball, or from a cushion. 2. A billiard game in which the table has no pockets and the cue ball is caromed from object balls and cushions.

CHALK: 1. Pool cue chalk is used to increase friction between the cue tip and the cue ball, virtually eliminating miscues. Chalk is produced from silica, pigmentations for color, and other compounds to hold it together and create density. Chalk's density affects its ability to transfer and stick to the cue tip. The denser the chalk the less likely it is to transfer; the softer, the more it will transfer, to the point of becoming messy. Cue chalk will also stain billiard cloth, so using a color that matches the cloth color is important. 2. A white cone chalk is used to keep a player's hand dry and slick. Its usefulness is questionable, and it is extremely messy if not used sparingly.

CUES: A pool cue can be junk or an expensive and personal accessory, ranging form throwaway to sentimentally overpriced. Cues are made as either one piece or two pieces that are joined when playing. Cues made in more than two pieces are not generally considered good quality or well made.

Good quality one-piece (house) cues are actually made from two pieces of wood. Maple is used for the shaft and rosewood, mahogany, maple, or some other hardwood for the butt. The two pieces are bonded together normally using a four-prong joint, but could have a flat face joint with the two halves pinned together.

The use of two pieces of wood is for more than decoration. Maple is used on the shaft for its hardness and trueness, while heavier woods are used for the butt to control the cue's weight distribution. Often, though, metal plugs or screws are inserted into the butt for added weight.

Cues are also made from graphite, fiberglass, aluminum, and other non-wood materials. Non-wood materials have come a long way in their ability to impart english on a cue ball, and the simple fact that they will not warp is a major advancement over wood. Still, the feel, consistent control, and beauty of wood cannot be duplicated.

The weights of cues range from 15 to 22 ounces. The best neutral cue weight is between 18 and 20 ounces. Cue weights are determined by an individual's preference, stroke, feel, and experience. There is no right or wrong weight or cue size, as long as the player is comfortable using the cue. A top quality shaft is always pro tapered to give it the same diameter from the cue tip back 10 to 12 inches toward the joint. This helps create a solid level stroke as the cue slides through a bridge. The diameters of a shaft at the tip, and along the pro taper, range from 11 to 14 millimeters. The ideal cue shaft size is said to be between 12 and 13 millimeters (1/2 inch). The real size criterion, however, is that a shaft should fit comfortably within a closed bridge (see *A Rookie's Guide to Playing Winning Pool* on **rookies-guide.com**).

CUE CASES: Cue cases are designed to carry and protect from one to several two-piece cues. They come in a variety of colors with shoulder straps and accessory pouches and pockets.
Soft cases are made of vinyl or soft leather and lined with cotton, foam, velvet, or such material. Hard cases are made from wood, aluminum, plastic, or leather. They are lined with cloth, wool, velvet, fleece, etc. Hard cases are generally considered superior to soft cases for storing a cue for long periods or transporting over long distances.

CUE JOINTS: A two-piece cue shaft is mechanically attached to the butt by a joint. There are four basic kinds of cue joints: double screw, single screw, implex, and quick release.

1. A double screw joint is a double metal screw that turns into a double metal lug. Both halves of the joint (collars) are metal, usually stainless steel, so that the joining face is metal to metal. The double screws, arranged one inside the other, makes an extremely stiff joint.

2. A single screw joint is a metal screw that turns into a metal lug. The two halves of the joint are metal and metal, plastic and metal, or plastic and plastic, with the metal screw in the center. This joint is stiff to medium stiff.

3. An implex joint is a metal screw that screws into a tapped hole in the end of the shaft, either directly into the wood or into a plastic or Lucite insert. The joining face of an implex joint can be plastic to wood, but is usually wood to wood, making this joint the most flexible.

4. The quick release is a stainless steel or titanium pin that slips into a retaining insert in the shaft. Two or three quick turns lock the shaft into place. The joining face is metal to plastic or fiber, or wood-to-wood, making the joint medium to flexible in stiffness.

CUE RACKS: Cue racks are designed to store cues in a vertical position to help prevent warping. Cue racks can be mounted to the wall or sat on the floor, depending on design. Racks can be as simple as two pieces of wood made to hold only six or so cues, to something elaborate that holds ten or twelve cues, balls, accessories, and drinks.

CUE TIPS: Cue tips are merely discs of tanned leather in some variance of compression from soft to hard. Some expensive tips are chemically treated with a finishing polish, compressed and calibrated for hardness. Some are infused with chalk to prevent miscuing, others are simply pressed, stamped leather and are not treated in any fashion. A vinyl or leather base is often bonded to the back of the tip to facilitate adhesion to the ferrule.

Soft tips take chalk better than hard, but hard tips have greater durability. Cuing the ball causes soft tips to compress and conform to the ball's shape, allowing for maximum contact. This makes soft tips more forgiving and less prone to miscuing. Hard tips, on the other hand, will not give or contort when they strike the cue ball. Hard tips must be chalked often, stroked with precision, and the cue ball must be hit closer to center to prevent miscuing.

CUSHION: The rubber attached to the inside of a rail and covered with cloth. The cushion is that part of the rail that rebounds the ball. The most common pool table profile is K-66.

CUSHION NOSE: That part of the cushion that contacts the ball.

DIAMOND: 1. One of 18 inlays one the top rail used to aid in shot making. 2. A nine-ball rack.

DUST COVER: Dust covers are used to protect the table's bed cloth and top rails from sunlight, pets, spills and thrills, and of course dust. So, when using the table for hobbies, changing baby's diapers, sorting dirty laundry, cleaning the carburetor, and so on, use a cover.

FACING: Laminated rubber and canvas, or cork attached to the end of the cushions to deaden the ball's rebound.

FEATHER STRIP: A wood or plastic strip that friction-holds the rail cloth into a groove at the top of the rail.

FELT: A matted material that is *not* used on pool tables. Although billiard cloth is often called felt, it is not. See Billiard Cloth.

FERRULE: A sleeve or point installed on the end of a cue shaft to prevent splitting or splintering. Ferrules are made of plastic, fiber, Lucite, or phenolic. Plastic ferrules are used on inexpensive cues, and Lucite or phenolic on higher priced custom cues. Fiber ferrules are generally used on one-piece house cues, but can be found on some inexpensive custom cues. The outside diameter of the ferrule will be the same as the cue shaft and tip, and the length can vary from $^1/_2$ inch to a little over 1 inch. Ferrules are usually installed onto a tenon cut into the end of the shaft, or onto metal screws that are implanted into the shaft end.

FOOT RAIL: The end rail at the rack end of the table. It is usually the end rail without the nameplate.

FRAME: That portion of a table that gives support to the slate.

FULL SIZE SLATE: A slate that extends beneath the rails, allowing the rails to be fastened securely to the slate.

GLOVE: Pool gloves are a recent addition to a player's arsenal, and they are as practical as they are gaudy. Pool gloves cover only the bridge fingers and are made of Polyester or nylon Spandex. They make the player's bridge as slick as powder without the mess. The cue shaft can be clamped tightly within a bridge and still slide with relative ease, eliminating the need for talc, powder, and cue cleaners. Initially, like most innovations of this type, they were shunned by "fashioned minded" players. But that is changing.

HEAD RAIL: The end rail at the break end of the table. It is usually the end rail that carries the nameplate.

HOME STYLE TABLE: A table made for the home; that is, noncommercial.

LEVELERS: Adjustable leveling pods attached to pool table feet.

MITERED CAPS: Plastic or metal trim that covers the rail ends where they join.

PLATFORM: See Slate platform.

POOL: A common name given to billiard games in general, and Pocket Billiards in particular.

PRO TAPER: The narrow end of a cue shaft that has the same diameter as the tip, extending backwards eight to ten inches.

RAIL CASTINGS: Metal castings that join the rails to each other.

RAIL CLOTH: The billiard cloth attached to the rails.

RE-COVER: The installation of new billiard cloth.

REGULATION: 1. Regulations are rules set by regulating bodies like the Billiard Congress of America (BCA). A regulation billiard table, for example, is what the regulating body determines it to be for a given tournament; it is not necessarily a nine-foot table.

SEAM: The connection joints of a multi-piece slate set.

SHIM: Flat or tapered stock used to level a billiard table.

SLATE PLATFORM: A stiff, flat (should be solid) board surface at the top of a cabinet or frame that serves as a bed for the slate.

SLIP-ON TIPS: Slip-on tips consist of a thin-shelled ferrule and tip that slip over the original ferrule, or bare shaft end.

SNOOKER: A billiard game played on a large table with six pockets, fifteen red balls, and six numbered balls.

STANDARD SIZE SLATE: Slate that ends beneath the cushion but still allows the rails to be attached to the slate, usually from the side.

TACKING BOARD: A board affixed to the bottom of the slate to provide a means of attaching the billiard cloth.

TACKING STRIP: The bottom portion of the rail used to attach the rail cloth to the rail.

TRIANGLE: A triangle (or fifteen ball rack) is a triangular shaped frame made of plastic or wood used for positioning a set of balls on the playing surface. Seven and nine ball racks are usually called diamonds.

UNDERSIZE SLATE: A slate that ends at the inner edge of the rails, usually beneath the cushion. The rails are attached to the frame and not the slate itself.

UNBACKED SLATE: Some slate is just slabs of rock with no backing. The slate is laid directly onto the slate platform, which may or may not double as a means of bed cloth attachment. Usually the cloth is glued to the slate.

ABOUT THE AUTHOR

After three years in the U.S. Army's 101st Airborne division (1962-1965) jumping out of perfectly good airplanes and working on Huey helicopters, I married, had two daughters then attended Indiana University's School of Business in Bloomington, Indiana.

After Indiana University, I opened a twenty-four-table poolroom in Indiana where I played on, sold, and serviced a variety of new, used, and antique tables.

Now in Arizona, I have remained in the billiard table service and repair business.